Praise for *Unleashing Your Dog*

"As always, Marc Bekoff and Jessica _____ _____ view. *Unleashing Your Dog* is a scholarly book that is also a _____ ___.l must-read for dogs' human companions. It will enrich their dog savvy and improve their dogs' quality of life by giving them the opportunity to experience life through their dogs' eyes — well, actually, their noses and ears. I loved this book."

— **Dr. Ian Dunbar,** author of *Before and After Getting Your Puppy*

"This insightful and thought-provoking book offers information about the inner lives of our dogs that educates while being immensely readable. Marc Bekoff and Jessica Pierce debunk myths (such as that dogs don't experience jealousy — yes, they do), and explain why off-leash time and opportunities to use their extraordinary senses are so vital to the well-being of our canine friends who are, essentially, living in captivity. This book is a must-read for everyone who wishes to understand dogs and build harmonious relationships with the dogs in their lives."

— **Lisa Tenzin-Dolma,** author and principal of the
International School for Canine Psychology & Behaviour

"In this remarkably informative, inspirational book, ethologist Marc Bekoff and ethicist Jessica Pierce explore ways we can improve the lives of the dogs we claim to love but too often hold in virtual captivity. Everyone who shares their life with a dog or is thinking of doing so will benefit from this book, as will the dogs. In unleashing their dog, readers might find that they have liberated themselves to once again take joy in small pleasures, like a dog running freely."

— **Mark Derr,** author of *Dog's Best Friend, A Dog's History of America,*
and *How the Dog Became the Dog*

"In our modern times it is so easy to forget that, despite all our efforts, our best friends have remained *dogs*! Marc Bekoff and Jessica Pierce provide a powerful eye-opener on this fact for all dog owners."

— **Dr. Ádám Miklósi,** head of ethology at Eötvös Loránd University
and director of the Family Dog Project

"This is not just another dog book. It's a dog manifesto! Written by two supremely gifted experts, *Unleashing Your Dog* reveals not only what your dog wants but *why*. You owe it to your dog to read this book!"

— **Sy Montgomery,** author of *The Soul of an Octopus* and *How to Be a Good Creature*

"Imagine having dogs stand up and tell you how to give them their best lives. While they can't (or, at least, it can be tricky to translate what they're saying), Marc Bekoff and Jessica Pierce can. This book beautifully uses the science of dogs to help dog people bring compassion to our lives with them."

— **Alexandra Horowitz,** head of the Dog Cognition Lab at Barnard College and author of *Inside of a Dog: What Dogs See, Smell, and Know* and *Being a Dog: Following the Dog Into a World of Smell*

"Marc Bekoff and Jessica Pierce — both superbly savvy, super dog-knowledgeable and dog-friendly PhDs — make a great team when it comes to helping us understand and provide properly for our dogs. In this glorious book, they urge us to consider dog ownership from the dogs' point of view, to 'walk in their paws,' so to speak. This book will ultimately ensure that your dog has a home for life and you have a much-loved and properly understood canine companion. Two paws up for this great work! Designed to inform and educate in an entertaining and easy-to-read format, it will help dogs and dog owners everywhere live richer lives."

— **Dr. Nicholas H. Dodman,** professor emeritus at Tufts University and author of *The Dog Who Loved Too Much* and *The Well-Adjusted Dog*

"*Unleashing Your Dog* is the go-to book for enriching the lives of dogs. With practical suggestions based on cutting-edge scientific research, Marc Bekoff and Jessica Pierce show how dogs can exercise their senses and bodies to enjoy life to its fullest in a human-dominated world. This easy-to-read guide will enlighten and entertain dog lovers everywhere."

— **Dr. Marty Becker, DVM,** author of *Your Dog: The Owner's Manual*

Unleashing
Your Dog

Also by Marc Bekoff and Jessica Pierce

The Animals' Agenda:
Freedom, Compassion, and Coexistence in the Human Age

Wild Justice: The Moral Lives of Animals

Unleashing Your Dog

A FIELD GUIDE TO GIVING YOUR CANINE COMPANION THE BEST LIFE POSSIBLE

Marc Bekoff and Jessica Pierce

New World Library
Novato, California

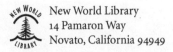

New World Library
14 Pamaron Way
Novato, California 94949

Text design by Tona Pearce Myers and Megan Colman

Library of Congress Cataloging-in-Publication Data

Names: Bekoff, Marc, author.
Title: Unleashing your dog : a field guide to giving your canine companion the best life possible / Marc Bekoff and Jessica Pierce.
Description: Novato, California : New World Library, [2019] | Includes bibliographical references and index.
Identifiers: LCCN 2018048490 (print) | LCCN 2018049190 (ebook) | ISBN 9781608685431 (e-book) | ISBN 9781608685424 (print : alk. paper)
Subjects: LCSH: Dogs--Behavior. | Dogs--Psychology.
Classification: LCC SF433 (ebook) | LCC SF433 .B445 2019 (print) | DDC 636.7--dc23
LC record available at https://lccn.loc.gov/2018048490

First printing, March 2019
ISBN 978-1-60868-542-4
Ebook ISBN 978-1-60868-543-1
Printed in Canada on 100% postconsumer-waste recycled paper

New World Library is proud to be a Gold Certified Environmentally Responsible Publisher. Publisher certification awarded by Green Press Initiative.

10   9   8   7   6   5   4   3

Contents

INTRODUCTION

Canine Captives

*U*nleashing Your Dog is a field guide to living with dogs in ways that enhance everyone's quality of life and that expand the freedom for dogs to really be dogs. Leashes are symbolic of our complicated relationship with our canine companions: They literally tie us together, one on each end. To people, the leash represents going out into the world with our dogs and giving them time to sniff, run, play, chase, have fun, roll, pee, poop, hump, and otherwise express themselves. To dogs, the leash likely represents these things, but it is also a tether that constrains their freedom because the leash is our means of control. It ensures that dogs are only allowed to go where we say, when we say, under our terms. Unleashing dogs means finding ways to let them have more freedom.

Most people who choose to share their home and heart with a dog do their best to provide a good life for their canine companion. We asked a number of people what they most value for their dog, and the two answers most commonly given were: "I want my dog to get to be a dog," and "I want my dog to be happy." These two values are closely linked. Most people want dogs to express dog behaviors, to be satisfied on

1

their own terms, and to "be themselves." This is important because a great deal of what we ask our pet dogs to do is un-dog-like and puts aside their doggy natures. For example, we ask them to sit inside alone for hours on end, and we ask them to walk slowly at the end of a rope instead of allowing them to dart here and there, deciding for themselves what deserves sniffing and exploring. We ask them not to bark, not to chase, not to hump, and not to sniff other dogs' butts. People who love dogs want their dog to be happy, and, to be happy, dogs need the freedom to act like dogs. Greater freedom means greater happiness.

Consider, for example, the experience of Marilyn and her rescue dog, Damien. Within a day of bringing Damien home, Marilyn realized that, she said, she'd "taken on a handful plus." She had completely underestimated how much she would have to change her life to accommodate her canine companion. She hadn't anticipated the depth and breadth of the commitment it required to give Damien what he wanted and needed, and she was "totally dumbfounded about what to do." How could she give this handsome guy the best life possible, given the constraints of her own life? After learning about dog behavior, Marilyn soon realized she'd have to adjust and give up some of her own "stuff" to give Damien what he needed. Damien was fully dependent on her for everything. But Marilyn also came to see that accommodating Damien in order to give him as much freedom as possible also enriched her own life. Though the changes she made felt like a sacrifice at first, she came to realize they weren't sacrifices at all because of what Damien gave her in return. Months later, Marilyn said that she and Damien were the happiest couple in the world. She admitted that she got pushed to the limit on occasion, and Damien's tolerance of her "humanness" was critical. He seemed to understand that she was doing the best she could and wanted him to be a happy dog.

Jim's experience with his young rescued mutt, Jasmine, was similar, except that Jasmine had been severely abused as a youngster. As Jim put it, "She was the most needy individual I'd ever met — canine, feline, or human." However, once Jim came to realize that he was Jasmine's lifeline, things changed. Jim worked hard to help Jasmine adapt to her life with Jim, and what began as an iffy relationship slowly evolved into one of mutual respect and trust. Jasmine helped Jim understand that dogs often struggle to adapt to human environments, particularly when dogs have had negative experiences with human caretakers.

Dog companions are captive animals, in that they are almost completely dependent on humans to provide for their physical, emotional, and social needs. This does not mean that dogs can't be happy in human homes, but rather, humans often have a good deal of work to do to ensure that their canine and other housemates live with as much freedom as possible. Fortunately, unleashing your dog, literally and metaphorically, is fun for all involved.

WHAT DOES "BEING CAPTIVE" MEAN?

Dogs are typically portrayed as happy-go-lucky members of our extended human families, without a care in the world. Indeed, the phrase "It's a dog's life" is sometimes used to describe days filled with indolence and pleasure. Aside from trained working dogs, all our dog companions do, after all, is sleep, laze around, eat, play, and hang out with friends. What could be easier, especially when someone reliably plops down a bowl of food several times a day? We are here to tell you that the lives of homed dogs aren't necessarily all fun and games, and that living as the companions of humans comes with some important compromises on the part of dogs. To adapt to human environments and expectations, dogs must sacrifice some of their "dogness." Despite our best efforts to provide a good life, and without quite realizing it, we usually ask them to live like *us* rather than like dogs. However, in order to successfully allow and even encourage our dogs to *be dogs*, we need to understand who dogs really are and how to help them express their dogness within our world.

When conservation biologist Susan Townsend, Marc's last doctoral student at the University of Colorado in Boulder, heard about this book, she told him that whenever she comes home to Angel, a Chihuahua mix, she asks, "How's my little prisoner doing?" Susan's greeting, although said in companionable jest, reflects an important reality.[1]

Our companion animals are not "held captive" the same way a tiger or gorilla is confined behind bars inside a zoo. They are not wild species who have been taken from their natural habitats and are being held against their will in a cage or artificial setting. But in important respects, companion dogs like Angel are also captive animals, and we are their captors. Maybe "captives and captors" sounds melodramatic and overly negative. After all, a good deal of the time humans and dogs share a beautiful, mutually pleasing interspecies relationship. But for just a minute, consider the constraints pet dogs face within a human home and a human-run world.

DEFINITION: CAPTIVE

According to the online Etymology Dictionary, the noun *captive* means "one who is taken and kept in confinement; one who is completely in the power of another." The word's roots come from the Latin *captivus*, "caught, taken prisoner," and from *capere*, "to take, hold, seize."

Simply put, "being captive" means that your life is not your own, that the contours of your daily existence are shaped by someone else. It doesn't necessarily mean that you are mistreated or unhappy or that your captors intend to harm or punish you. Being captive refers to a type of existence, not its quality. It means being confined to a certain space, one not necessarily of your choosing. It means you lack the ability to choose what you do, who you see, who and what you smell, and what and when you eat. It means, at times, being forced to do certain tasks others ask of you. It means depending on someone else to provide the basic necessities of life, like food and shelter, along with opportunities for meaningful engagement with others and the world. In these ways, dogs kept as pets are captive animals, and humans are their captors because we control all these aspects of their lives.

This is easy to appreciate if we turn the tables. Do dogs go to the people store or the people shelter and choose which human they'll take home? Do dogs, if they decide that they don't really like the human they have chosen, get to return their person and bring home another one who is more attractive and better behaved? Do dogs determine when and what humans eat, how often humans get to pee and where, and which friends they can see? Do dogs put humans on a leash so they won't run too fast, go too far, or greet others they think the human shouldn't?

Of course, this is ridiculously far-fetched, but would we put up with the conditions under which pet dogs live in our society? Absolutely not. We'd never give up control over the most basic aspects of our lives. No matter how benevolently we govern our dogs, we nevertheless ask them, and often command them, to live under our rules, within our kingdom.

This is the crucial starting point for understanding our relationships with, and our responsibilities toward, our furry friends. No matter how loving human caretakers are, companion dogs must cope with an asymmetrical relationship. To live in our world, we require them to give up some of their freedoms and natural canine behaviors. In her book *Love Is All You Need*, service-dog trainer Jennifer Arnold writes that dogs live in an environment that "makes it impossible for them to alleviate their own stress and anxiety." She explains: "In modern society, there is no way for our dogs to keep themselves safe, and thus we are unable to afford them the freedom to meet their own needs. Instead, they must depend on our benevolence for survival."[2] Think about it. We teach dogs that, in order to pee or poop, they must get our attention and ask for permission to go outside the house. When dogs do go outside, we often restrain them with a leash or within a fence and tell them, "Don't pee or poop there." Dogs eat what and when we feed them, and they're scolded if they eat what or when we say they shouldn't. Dogs play with the toys we give them, and they get in trouble for choosing their own toys (which we mysteriously call "shoes" or "the television remote"). Most of the time our schedules and preferences determine our dog's playmates and friendships. All things considered, it's a very one-sided relationship that no adult human would tolerate.

Some people claim that, because of domestication, dogs are conditioned to accept, and are content with, these asymmetries in our relationship. They argue that the long association with humans has changed what is "natural" for dogs, and in some ways, this is true. By definition, a domestic dog is not a wild species, and their behavior reflects what we've asked from them in the past and our own expectations. Nevertheless, dogs are not four-legged humans, either, and they are not completely adapted to human environments, as anyone who lives with a dog knows firsthand. Dogs retain elements of "wildness" and behaviors that resemble those of their wild wolf ancestors. Indeed, many of these traits we value highly, and we wouldn't want them to disappear, such as their devotion to their family group, their sociability, and their willingness to help and protect. Dogs will never fit easily and without negotiation into human homes and lifestyles, and that's the way it is. For example, dogs will always need to be carefully taught to walk on a leash, not to chase prey, and not to roam the neighborhood in search of a nice-smelling mating partner. Of course, the fact that dog trainers and veterinary behaviorists are in such high demand indicates that numerous dogs need a lot of help trying to live successfully with and among humans.

In other words, living with dogs involves a careful balance. Some constraints are essential for the safety of dogs and humans, and yet if we aren't careful and extremely attentive to what our dog needs, these constraints can severely compromise our dog's quality of life and ability to thrive. One goal of this book is to examine and become aware of the constraints we place on dogs, to identify those that are unnecessarily strict and those that are so subtle that we might not even realize we're depriving our dogs of freedoms they need or want.

You might say, with dogs, we have made a kind of Faustian bargain: To bring dogs into our lives and love them, we have had to compromise their freedoms and, in some ways, compromise their well-being. Instead of seeking knowledge, like Faust, we want love and companionship. We want to capitalize on the shared emotions that form a social glue — that celebrated "bond" — between humans and dogs.[3] But the price of this love and companionship is that we make our truest companions into beings different from and less than themselves. Our hope is that this book helps you see and address this ethical quandary to improve the life of the dog, or dogs, you love.

UNLEASHING DOGS, ENHANCING FREEDOMS

Words are important and have power. There is a reason we don't call companion animals *captives* nor their humans *captors*. These negative words don't reflect the nature of our intentions or feelings for dogs. Similarly, we don't like the word *owner*, which objectifies dogs and encourages us, by implication, to treat dogs like property that can be owned, used, and discarded. We prefer terms like *guardian* or *companion* rather than *owner*. Even though our society legally defines dogs as property, we don't have to use that language, treat them that way, or think of ourselves in those terms. Dogs are conscious beings with thoughts and feelings, just like us, which is why we never use the pronouns *that* or *it* when referring to dogs, since these refer to objects. We prefer to use *he*, *she*, and *they* and *who* or *whom*.

Further, since *captivity* and *freedom* can be loaded words — ones that carry judgment and whose meanings or understandings vary depending on the context — we prefer the terms *deprivations* and *enhancements* when talking about dog well-being. We'll explore these concepts further in the field guide, but here are the basics: A deprivation means not letting dogs do something "natural" that they are highly motivated and driven to do. An enhancement is an intervention that increases a dog's freedom to be a dog. Enhancements can be things we provide, like unclicking the leash and allowing dogs to run hard and zoom around without a care in the world. Enhancements can also be things from which we protect dogs, such as fear, pain, sensory overload, unwanted petting, and danger.

The antidote for captivity is freedom. Clearly, there is a basic tension between captivity and freedom, and dogs exist within this zone of uncertainty. Although dogs are captive (there's no getting around this), they can nevertheless enjoy remarkable degrees of freedom within human environments.

Like captivity, freedom isn't black and white, but rather comes in shades of gray. Dogs in our society live under a whole range of conditions, and they experience varying levels of captivity-related stress and varying levels of freedom. Further, the way homed dogs live varies widely across the globe and even house to house. It's hard to speak in generalities, since there are always variations and exceptions. More to the point: Each dog and each person is different. Each dog experiences certain deprivations more keenly, and each person will find certain enhancements and freedoms easier to provide than others. Our hope with this book is a simple one: We hope it helps you discover many ways to provide your dog with more freedom and less captivity, however you can. Every dog deserves the best life we can offer, and this "best life" means giving them the greatest amount of freedom and the fewest experiences of captivity-induced deprivation we can provide.

TEN FREEDOMS FOR DOGS

The "Five Freedoms" are a popular cornerstone of animal welfare. First developed in 1965 and formalized in 1979 by the UK's Farm Animal Welfare Council, the Five Freedoms were designed to address some of the worst welfare problems experienced by animals used within industrial farming (or "factory farming"). Since their development, the Five Freedoms have been applied to an increasingly broad range of captive animals, such as those living in zoos and research labs. Over the past few years, the Five Freedoms have also made their way into discussions of companion animal welfare. They provide a good starting point for thinking about enhancing freedoms for dogs. We've adapted and expanded the original Five Freedoms into Ten Freedoms that should guide our interactions with dogs.

Freedoms one to five focus on freedoms *from* uncomfortable or aversive experiences. Freedoms six to ten focus on freedoms *to be dogs*.

Like all animals, dogs need the following:

1. Freedom from hunger and thirst
2. Freedom from pain
3. Freedom from discomfort
4. Freedom from fear and distress
5. Freedom from avoidable or treatable illness and disability
6. Freedom to be themselves
7. Freedom to express normal behavior
8. Freedom to exercise choice and control
9. Freedom to frolic and have fun
10. Freedom to have privacy and "safe zones"

Even the most well-cared-for dogs — those who are doted upon, have soft beds and tasty nutritional food, and get good veterinary care — may experience deprivations of which their owner is largely unaware.[4] This is because a great many people who choose to share their home with a dog don't know very much about dog behavior. One report on pet owners' knowledge of dog behavior, for example, found that 13 percent of people had done no research into dog behavior prior to acquiring a dog, and only 33 percent felt "very informed" about the basic welfare needs of dogs.[5] Although some dog owners have read shelves full of books about the natural history, ethology, and care of dogs, many others just fly by the seat of their pants. Dogs are amazingly adaptive and resilient and find ways to survive even in environments that aren't particularly dog friendly. But obviously, most people want their dogs to thrive, not just scrape by, and the best way to help them do that is to learn as much as possible about who dogs really are and what they need from us.

Evidence from trainers, dog psychologists, and veterinarians clearly shows that far too many dogs are not getting what they need and suffer from varying degrees of stress. Millions of dogs are plagued by boredom, frustration, and anxiety. These negative feelings often manifest in what owners mistakenly perceive as "behavioral problems" in their dogs, whether it be destroying furniture when left alone during the day, obsessive barking, hyperactivity, or overeating. These issues make clear that taking care of a dog's basic needs — providing fresh water, nutritious food, exercise, appropriate housing, and adequate veterinary care — is just the starting point. Like humans, dogs also need emotional connection and support and to be engaged with their world. They need to socialize with other dogs and humans. They need ample opportunities in nature, exercising their senses the same way they exercise their muscles. They need to stretch their bodies and minds and feel challenged.

Does providing this require compromise on our part? Yes, it usually does, but it doesn't need to be overwhelming, either. Often, the most important change is shifting perspective, paying more careful attention to our dogs, and enhancing the freedoms we already provide so they are as meaningful to our dogs as possible. Take, for example, the morning walk. Most people have limited time before work to walk their dog, and no matter how much a dog might enjoy a sixty-minute ramble, that's not going to happen. So make the time you have really count. After reading this book, think about the morning walk from your dog's point of view and ask: *What does my dog most need and want?* Give them that.

COMMAND CENTRAL!

Come! Sit! Stay! Don't!

One of the ways humans control dogs is by issuing commands. Some poor dogs are subjected to so many commands during a day that it is a wonder they remain sane. In fact, people are often advised by trainers that their dog should be commanded to do just about everything — a dog should have to perform some trick or obey some command for each kibble they eat and each ball they chase. But the overcommanding and obsessive-compulsive controlling of our dogs is not the best way to enhance their sense of independence and autonomy.

After visiting many dog parks and other places where people and dogs hang out, our impression is that people say *no* much more than *yes* or "good dog" and that praise occurs much less often, especially spontaneously. Marc did an informal study at one of the local dog parks in which he recorded three hundred instances in which people talked to their or someone else's dog. He found that 83 percent of the time people said something to stop dogs from doing something, and only 17 percent of the time did they say something positive. And of the fifty-one times that they said something positive, only 6 percent of the time was something such as "good dog" said spontaneously, when the dogs were just being dogs and doing what dogs do.[6]

There's an upside to giving our dogs more freedoms: We reap benefits, too. Happy and contented dogs tend to be easier to live with, resulting in happier and more contented guardians. "Problem" canine behaviors related to anxiety or frustration can resolve themselves, giving us more time to enjoy our friendship with our canine companions. People sometimes fall into bad habits of complaining about how difficult dogs are to care for and live with. At dog parks, we've heard numerous people say something like, "Gosh, I've had to change my whole day around taking her to a dog park." But you know who else experiences more freedom and satisfaction when we unleash our dogs more often? We do. Letting go of the leash is a benefit that helps everyone.

BECOMING FLUENT IN DOG

Dogs are everywhere in our world — in our neighborhoods, in our cars, and in our homes. Yet in some important ways, we often don't really *notice* dogs. We see them as ornamentation for our own human drama, not appreciating who dogs really are and what this world is like from their perspective.

The key to being able to provide dogs with enhanced freedom is to understand how they sense their world — what the world looks like, smells like, feels like, tastes like, and sounds like to them. Only by understanding how dogs experience the world will we be able to understand the ways in which human environments compromise their welfare and be able to find ways to compensate. To do this, we need to get inside the heads, hearts, and sense organs of our furry friends. That's the heart of what we hope this book provides.

For a long time, scientists ignored dogs and dog behavior because dogs weren't seen as candidates for serious study. Dogs were considered artifacts created by humans, and not real or "natural" animals in their own right. Dogs were of course used as models to study other things (diseases, for example), but they were not seen as animals of interest in and of themselves. All this began to change, and change dramatically, about two decades ago, and now the sciences of canine cognition and emotion are growing by leaps and bounds. Some still refer to studies of the cognitive and emotional lives of dogs as "soft science," a reflection of the stubborn prejudice against dogs and against the scientific study of animal minds and animal feelings. But attitudes are starting to evolve, as the importance of canine science becomes established. Rigorous studies of dog cognition are producing large amounts of detailed data, some of which are already being put to work to make the lives of dogs and their humans better. We know, for example, that dogs have evolved complex cognitive abilities and they experience a wide range of emotions. Yet much remains to be done.

Given the huge number of dog books and training manuals available at bookstores and online, and the thousands of websites dedicated to dogs and dog behavior, it may surprise you to learn how many gaps there are in our collective knowledge about dogs. We really don't know as much about dogs as many writers imply. As you'll see throughout this book, when it comes to this or that topic, we are often forced to concede, "There just isn't very much research."

Even as rigorous canine science continues to grow, myths and pop science still abound. One of the challenges for dog owners is being able to separate the wheat from the chaff and identify areas where the science is solid and where it is not. This can be challenging, since new canine science emerges daily, even with books like this to help! For example, one prevailing myth is that dogs don't experience complex emotions such as jealousy or guilt. However, new evidence disputes this. For instance, a neuroimaging study by Dr. Peter Cook and his colleagues showed that the same part of the brain in both dogs and humans lights up when they're feeling jealous. For individuals of both species, there is increased activation of the amygdala.[7]

We need to understand what dogs are feeling not only to make sure that their behavioral needs are being met but also to communicate clearly with them. Successfully training dogs to live with us will be far more effective if based on accurate canine science. For example, what should we do if we come home to a ravaged garbage can and find our dog cowering in the corner with ears folded down. Our dog looks "guilty," as if our dog understands they've done something wrong, so we may be tempted to punish our dog, perhaps with a loud verbal scolding along with a "scruffing," which involves grabbing the loose fur on a dog's neck, rolling them onto their back, and holding them down as if to say, "I am the boss!" Jennifer Arnold calls this the "because I said so (BISS) technique" of training and notes that it fails and doesn't result in "a fair and mutually beneficial relationship."[8]

However, can we be sure we understand what our dog understands, and is punishment the most effective response? Many people assume that the "hang dog" facial expression, with ears pressed down, is an admission of wrongdoing, but we really don't know whether dogs feel guilt — the jury is still out on this question. Even though it's likely that dogs do, their understanding of right and wrong probably differs from ours, and we might be misreading our dog's facial expression and body posture, which is common. Our dog might be expressing fear, stress, or confusion, rather than guilt, and our punishment might only increase those feelings without reinforcing the correct behavior. Scruffing, for its part, is a training method based upon inaccurate assumptions about dominance hierarchies and punishment. Physically punishing dogs when they've done something wrong or something we don't like, whether by scruffing or with a smack on the nose, doesn't really work to change their behavior.[9] As dog training expert Peter Vollmer notes, "Excessive punishment, especially when administered sometime after undesirable behavior occurs, can lead to undesirable side effects such as avoidance of the owner, constant subordinate signaling, and stress-related physiologic problems."[10]

LITTLE WOLVES?

Many people believe that if we understand wolves, then we will get a good handle on what dogs want and need to thrive. After all, domestic dogs evolved from wild wolf ancestors, and they remain close enough genetically to be able to crossbreed. However, although wolf behavior is interesting, it isn't necessarily an accurate template for thinking about our dogs. There are many ways in which thinking of our dogs as little wolves, or domesticated wolves, may mislead us as we try to understand what our dogs really need and how best to interact with them. For instance, wolves typically form well-organized packs with well-defined dominance hierarchies and divisions of labor, whereas dogs don't. Wolves also commonly mark territorial boundaries, but dogs only rarely do so.

Becoming fluent in dog also means being aware of, and sensitive to, the specific situation or context in which we are interacting with our dog. As with people, a dog's behavior can change depending on the situation or social context. This is actually a significant limitation in many dog studies. The behavior of dogs living in a cage inside of a research lab is constrained and shaped by this environment, and behavior patterns observed in the lab don't necessarily translate into, say, a shelter environment, where the stimuli are quite different. Then, of course, the behavior of dogs in a shelter will be different from behavior in a home, in a dog park, and in a doggy day care, and each of these from one another. Behavior at the veterinarian's office may be a world unto itself. Further, each shelter, home, and veterinarian's office is its own microcosm. Plus, many human guardians report that their dog is "leash reactive." Slap on a leash and their otherwise perfectly amiable dog becomes aggressive toward other dogs who walk past. As you can see, behavior doesn't occur in a vacuum, though it's often assumed that it does.

Above all, we know relatively little about the behavior of dogs in human home environments, although this is perhaps the most important context within which it would be useful to know what our dogs are thinking, feeling, and wanting.[11] Indeed, we need to learn about dogs in the places in which they live and spend time to help them develop what Niki Tudge, founder and president of the Pet Professional Guild, calls "lifestyle relevant skills."[12] Of course, it would be very difficult to design a study of "home behavior" that could be generalized to all dogs, since each human home environment is unique. But that shouldn't stop you from studying your own dog in your home. Your research conclusions might not apply to all dogs, but they will apply to the most important dog in your life — your own. We encourage you to study and observe for yourself how your dog navigates your shared home and to continue observing your dog in every setting and notice what changes and what doesn't.

MAKING AND USING ETHOGRAMS

This book will help you become fluent in dog by inviting you to become an ethologist-in-training.[13] An ethologist is someone who studies the behavior of animals, usually in their natural habitat. You can use the science of ethology to help you explore who your dog is and what he or she wants and needs. For example, you can learn your dog's unique likes and dislikes, coping styles, learning styles, and individual quirks.

One thing you can do is to make ethograms of your dog's behavior. An ethogram is a kind of menu of what animals do, and it forms the cornerstone of behavioral studies. You can create an ethogram in several different environments, such as at home, at the dog park, or on the evening walk around the neighborhood and compare them to one another. You might make an ethogram of your dog interacting with other dogs or interacting with you or with other humans. You can make an ethogram of other dogs, too, so you can compare the behavior patterns of different dogs. By carefully watching and cataloging your dog's behavior, you can learn how their behavior changes from one setting to another. Developing an ethogram is fun and opens a window into learning about how animals behave. It's often considered the first and most important stage of scientific research.

Numerous dog ethograms are available that you can use to get ideas for developing an ethogram for your own dog. Two particularly good examples are provided in books by ethologists Roger Abrantes (*Dog Language*) and Michael W. Fox (*Behaviour of Wolves, Dogs, and Related Canids*). Barbara Handelman's *Canine Behavior: A Photo Illustrated Handbook* also is an excellent resource, as is "Learning to Speak Dog Part 4: Reading a Dog's Body" on the Tails from the Lab website. All are listed in the bibliography.

Some behavior patterns that you might score include a dog's approach to other dogs (speed and orientation); biting directed toward different parts of the body; biting intensity (inhibited and soft, or hard and accompanied by either shaking of the head or not); rolling over; standing over; chin resting; play soliciting; self-play; peeing and the posture used; pooping; growling; barking; whining; approaching and withdrawing; pawing directed toward different parts of the body; ear position; tail position; gait; and so on. Marc and his students have discovered that the behavior of most dogs can be accounted for by scoring around fifty different behavior patterns.

Splitters and lumpers: Depending on their focus, researchers tend to approach or organize their data in two ways, either by splitting or lumping. Splitters do microanalyses of actions, whereas lumpers are interested in broad categories of behavior, such as play, aggression, and mating. Whether you split or lump actions depends on the questions in which you're interested. We would recommend splitting first, since then you can lump later if that seems like the best strategy. For instance, rather than simply writing "bite," distinguish where the bite occurred and note it as a face bite, ear bite, neck bite, body bite, and so on. Or you can indicate intensity by noting an intense hip slam versus a mild hip slam. You can group all bites or hip slams together later, but you will lose the subtle differences if you do not split them as you're compiling your ethogram. Marc always has been a splitter in his studies of dogs and their wild relatives, and it was because of this that he found that after fifty different actions had been identified, the probability of adding a new behavior was very rare.

To put this all together, the simple steps in constructing an ethogram are as follows: watch animals in person or on videos; list each different behavior pattern and vocalization; compare your list with others; watch more and write down additional behavior patterns and vocalizations; come up with a code for each behavior so you can "score" observations easily; and split behaviors rather than lumping two or more together.

Dogs also show individual differences in their

time and activity budgets. So, using your mobile phone or a stopwatch, you can gather information not only on what they do but on how much time they spend engaged in different activities. Changes in what they do and how much time they spend doing different things can be used as indicators of how dogs are feeling.

Just as context is highly variable, so too is the behavior of each individual dog. Many variables can influence behavior, including genetics, upbringing, breed, learning, cognitive style, and personality.[14] Clearly, an individual's prior experiences also influence their behavior, as do expectations or thoughts about the future. This is a point to which we'll return repeatedly; namely, it's essential to know your dog as the individual he or she is. What works for Rosco might not work for Freddie, and what works for Maybell might not work for Ellie.

A useful perspective to take when considering our dog is as someone from a different culture, like a foreign-exchange student. Our home and culture have similarities to our dog's (we feel similar emotions and have similar physical sensations), but there are significant differences. We speak different languages, and physical gestures might mean different things (as when a nodding head means "no" in one culture and "yes" in another). Just as we help an exchange student succeed by closely working with them to bridge any cultural differences and find commonalities, we can help our dogs by providing this same kind of cultural awareness and sensitivity. Our foreign-exchange student doesn't need to learn English to live happily and peacefully in our home, and the same is true for our dog. Despite a language barrier, dogs are highly adept at communicating with humans (as research into dog social cognition has shown), and we have the same ability to understand and become fluent in dog, so we can interpret our dog's behavior and communicate clearly.

ECOLOGICAL RELEVANCE AND YELLOW SNOW

Within the field of animal behavior, the phrase *ecological relevance* means studying animals in ways that account for their sensory and motor skills. In other words, we can't expect species to respond to stimuli or in ways that they aren't capable of or that don't come naturally. For example, asking an animal who can't hear high-pitched ultrasounds to discriminate between two stimuli using ultrasound is not ecologically relevant.

What does *ecological relevance* mean when observing our dogs? Don't expect them to do things that are beyond their motor or sensory capacities, and don't assume dogs use their same five senses the way humans do. Here's an example. One of the methods designed by researchers to assess the capacity for self-recognition in other species is called the mirror test. Without the animal knowing, a mark (such as a red dot) is placed on the animal's forehead, and the animal is placed in front of a mirror. If the animal responds to the red dot, such as by trying to rub it off using self-directed movements, then researchers conclude that the individual recognizes themself in the mirror and knows the dot is on their body. Some chimpanzees, elephants, dolphins, and magpies do this.

Dogs consistently fail this test, so some researchers have claimed that dogs don't have the cognitive capacity for self-recognition. But the mirror test simply isn't ecologically relevant for dogs. Dogs have eyes. They can see the dot. But dogs don't rely as heavily on visual signals as they do on olfactory signals, and it may be that self- and other-recognition in dogs is primarily through smell. When Marc studied self-recognition by observing how his dog Jethro responded to his own "yellow snow" (compared to the urine-soaked snow from other dogs), Jethro showed he preferred the yellow snow of other dogs. Additional research into olfactory self-recognition in dogs confirms that dogs likely understand "me" as distinct from "you" when this question is asked in ecologically relevant terms for dogs.[15]

WALKING IN THEIR PAWS

One of the most important messages in *Unleashing Your Dog* is that there is no universal "dog." Each dog is a unique individual with unique needs and a unique personality. As Ray Pierotti and Brandy Fogg note in their book *The First Domestication: How Wolves and Humans Coevolved*, the word *dog* is difficult to define and "domestic dogs are a grab-bag assemblage of individuals."[16] Of course, there is no universal "human," either, and trying to understand the motivations and perceptions of the human side of the dog-human equation is also essential.

Trying to think and feel our way through our dog's daily life *from the dog's perspective* is a useful exercise. As our dog's companion, we can train ourselves to be attentive to our dog's experiential world, to walk in their paws and imagine what's happening in their head and heart. As with parenting, love is not enough. We also need logic. We need to become dog literate and understand who dogs are, what they need, and what their behavior can tell us about how they are feeling.

HUMAN AND DOG CULTURAL COMPARISONS

Human Culture	Dog Culture
Butts and groins are private areas and not to be touched or smelled by strangers.	Sniffing butts and groins is perfectly natural behavior. It's like greeting someone by saying, "How do you do?" and getting the answer.
Humping is a perverted, inappropriate sexual behavior, and not something to do in public.	Humping is interesting and does not need to be private. All dogs do it, and it doesn't matter with what — a human leg, couch pillow, or whatever.

Barking is loud and annoying. Good dogs don't bark.	Barking is one of the main ways in which dogs communicate with one another and with us. They bark in a wide variety of contexts, including when they're playing, afraid, agitated, trying to get attention, and excited.
Dogs shouldn't chase bikes or squirrels, and they're naughty if they don't listen to commands and stop.	Dogs have a natural prey drive; since any quickly moving object might be prey, dogs often chase to find out.
When a dog refuses to obey a command and do what a person wants, the dog is being willfully stubborn and obstinate.	Dogs may hesitate or resist commands out of fear, nervousness, or confusion. They react to nonverbal communication as much as words, and if a person says one thing but indicates another with their tone, emotion, or body language, dogs may struggle to understand what's meant.
Hugging a dog is a sign of love.	When hugged by a person, dogs can sometimes feel trapped.
If a dog won't play with other dogs, that dog is anti-social or has a problem.	Dogs have preferences and a need for solitude just like people; dogs don't always like other specific dogs, or they prefer other activities to playing and socializing.

We also need to remember that dogs are not people. Yes, this is obvious. But it's also easy to forget, especially when our dogs form such close friendships with us that it feels like we do speak the same language and share the same understandings.

We need to tailor enhancements to fit the needs of our specific dog. A dog is never too young or too old for us to be thinking about ways to enhance their freedoms. Socialization is an especially important freedom enhancer for puppies. When puppies are not socialized, their freedoms are curtailed for the rest of their lives because they don't learn how to be "normal," well-adjusted dogs.[17] As ethologist and dog trainer Ian Dunbar suggests, puppies should be introduced to a hundred dogs and a hundred people before they're twelve weeks old. Of course, this is virtually impossible to do, but it's sage advice to ensure that puppies have plenty of contact with other dogs and with people other than their human companion. Also, puppies and dogs of all ages need to be cognitively challenged, and this extends well into their sunset years. Cognitively challenging work can have positive effects on the canine brain throughout the dog's lifespan. For example, lifelong training appears to be linked with increased attention span in aging dogs.[18]

GIVING DOGS THE BEST POSSIBLE LIVES

Bringing a dog into one's home is a decision with far-reaching ethical consequences. In adopting, buying, or otherwise acquiring a dog, we become responsible for the well-being of another living creature. We have a great deal of control over how much freedom our dogs experience, and to a large extent, our daily actions determine whether our dog enjoys a happy and full life. Yes, choosing to share your life with a dog is an awesome responsibility.

If you are already a guardian to a dog, think about what kind of human companion you ideally want to be for your canine friend. As you read this book, consider the ways that you can give your dog the very best life possible. None of us is perfect; no one ever lives up to their ideal all the time. But try to see the world through your dog's eyes (and their nose, tongue, paws, and skin!), and imagine all the little and big ways you can help your dog thrive. This is, after all, what you signed up for.

Our relationships with dogs are grounded in and guided by personal values. Sometimes these are openly acknowledged, and sometimes they are unstated but reflected in our actions. People differ in how they choose to live with their nonhuman companions, but it is useful to make these values explicit if you have invited another animal into your life or plan to do so. The first question is the one we pose above: What do you consider to be a good life for your dog, and how can you help your dog achieve this kind of life? Make a list of your goals; write them down.

As we've said, "unleashing your dog" is both literal — dogs need more time off leash — and metaphorical. We need to continually work toward increasing the freedoms that our dogs experience, thereby unleashing their potential to live life to the fullest. And with that, let's unclip the leash and begin enhancing the lives of the dogs we love so much.

Minnie, unleashed in the mountains of western Colorado.
Photo by Sophie Rae Gordon.

THE FIELD GUIDE TO FREEDOMS

Exercising and Enhancing the Senses

I f it's true that dogs are captive animals — because their experience of the world is largely, if not totally, influenced by what we, their caregivers, provide for them — then we can make our dogs' lives better by improving their environments and interactions in their terms. We can protect them from the stressful aspects of human environments, allow them as much freedom as possible to be themselves, and empower them to make choices and express their preferences.

Let's see what this means in daily practice.

For all animals, including dogs, one defining aspect of "captivity" is that it is restrictive and separate from the environment in which the species evolved. Thus, many of the stimuli captive animals are exposed to are unnatural or novel (to them), and these unusual stimuli can elicit a fight-or-flight stress response, one the animal may not be able to adequately express because of captivity. To improve your dog's life, think carefully about any sensory stimuli that cause stress and eliminate them. Enhancing our dogs' freedom includes protecting them from unwelcome or uncomfortable sensory experiences.

Captive animals also may lack opportunities to engage in evolved behavior patterns typical of their species, ones they are "hardwired" to perform. When captive environments are monotonous and barren, they don't allow animals to use their exquisitely evolved cognitive and sensory capacities, and this can lead to frustration and stress. For example, birds whose natural food-gathering behavior involves scratching the ground to find seeds will still "need" to scratch the ground, even if the ground is a concrete floor. When these types of evolved behavioral needs go unmet, individuals frequently engage in a wide range of unnatural behaviors, such as stereotyped pacing and self-destructive acts. Since human environments are frequently understimulating for dogs, we can also enhance their freedom by providing dogs with opportunities to exercise all their senses and reduce boredom through what are called "enrichments."[1] There's a good deal of evidence that even simple enrichments can make animals happier and less stressed out.

To summarize, there are two powerful ways to improve the lives of dogs:

1. Reduce the number of situations or stimuli that cause distress. This includes "aversive stimuli" — unpleasant sounds, smells, and physical sensations, such as feeling trapped — and failing to provide outlets for natural behaviors that dogs are highly motivated to perform. We call these "freedom inhibitors" or "deprivations."

2. Provide positive enrichments that stimulate the senses and provide opportunities for physical, psychological,

and social engagement with the world. We call these "freedom enhancers" or "enhancements."

If we think of captivity as a disease, one that causes unhealthy physical and emotional symptoms, then increased freedoms would be the antidote or remedy. Many of these are cheap, and none require a veterinarian's prescription. Mostly, they only require us to proactively help our canine companions by looking for the ways our home environments might be hard on our dogs and addressing them: by offering dogs more choice, more stimulation, more engagement, more freedoms.

The rest of this book is a "field guide" to the five major sensory experiences of dogs: smell, taste, touch, sight, and hearing. For each, we feature the freedom-enhancing "interventions" you can provide for your dog; you might think of these as ways to "free" the canine senses. Obviously, some topics or behavioral issues involve multiple senses. Dogs respond to what ethologists call "composite signals" that contain potential information from several senses. While the book discusses each sense separately, that's not how dogs use them in the real world.

However, by focusing on each sense, we use the science of how dogs experience and interact with the world to help you understand your dog's point of view. Understanding the senses individually, and how they work together, helps us understand some of the challenges of being a dog in a human-centered world. Senses are connected to feelings, and if dogs are encouraged to have positive and interesting sensory experiences, they will likely experience an increase in their overall happiness — which is what we want!

Like a field guide, this book is meant to be a reference, one that describes each sense and its characteristics and then provides the most important enhancements we can give dogs. Similar to a field guide to plants, say — which will "key out" specimens, classifying or identifying them by certain characteristics, such as the type of leaf, the color of their flower, the height of the plant, and so forth — this book "keys out" your dog by looking at the different senses. In each section, a short introduction overviews the sense and then provides a list of ways you can enhance this sensory domain for your dog. Skip around and turn to the topics that are most relevant for you and your dog, as you would with any field guide.

Many of the enhancements we propose aren't new. People who study dog cognition have been talking and writing about them for years. However, ongoing research focusing on canine behavior, cognition, emotions, and sensory physiology is generating a good deal of new information that has practical importance, and new data are constantly emerging. In many instances we integrate this new science into enhancements that may not yet have received much airtime.

We also try to bridge the gap that exists between the theoretical realm of canine cognitive science and the application of this research into the practical realm of dog teaching and training. That such a knowledge translation gap exists is understandable, given how much information is currently being generated by researchers all over the world. Like any field guide, this book captures the state of what we know right now about helping dogs adapt to human environments, but it will eventually need updating as new research expands, clarifies, and confirms what we know about dogs.[2]

CAVEATS:
WHEN THE LEASH IS NEEDED

If, while reading this book, you become tempted to throw away your dog's leash, here are two reminders why a leash is still at times useful and necessary: human etiquette and your canine companion's safety.

Etiquette: Often the rules of human etiquette run counter to what dogs want, and we must curtail their freedom for the sake of maintaining friendly relations, not only with other dogs, but also with other people, whether our neighbors, our houseguests, or strangers on the street. A dog may, for example, really want to pee on the neighbor's heirloom tomato plant; they may want to run free through the streets of town, greeting every human and dog in sight. Guardians must be attentive to and balance the needs of their dog *and* the needs of people. It's counterproductive not to, or else others may experience dogs as troublesome, unwelcome pests and want to curtail their freedoms even further. Responsible dog guardians build community goodwill that benefits dogs and everyone in the long run.

Safety: It's also essential to balance freedom with safety. As with human children, we need to avoid helicopter parenting and allow our dogs opportunities to make their own decisions and take risks, but within the constraints of parental supervision and good sense. Both children and dogs lack the experience and insight to appropriately judge risks or to anticipate what adults might consider obvious dangers, like busy roads. Balancing freedom with safety can surely lead to a better life for dogs and humans alike.

THE IMPORTANCE OF DOG TRAINING AND TEACHING

On the surface, it may seem counterintuitive, but one of the most important ways to increase freedom for your dog is to take training very seriously. When approached the right way, training isn't about controlling your dog's behavior but about you teaching your dog to function successfully with you in your home and in human environments in general. Training techniques create a method of communication between you and your dog, one you both learn and understand together.

This book is not a training manual per se, but throughout we explore how positive training can contribute to a dog's quality of life.

Here are some tips for approaching training in the most effective way:

- Dog training is as much about teaching yourself as it is about teaching your dog. Educate yourself about dog behavior and training techniques.
- The minute you bring a dog into your home, the teaching begins, whether the dog is a puppy or an adult. Puppies are eager to soak up information, if it is presented with patience and in ways appropriate to their age and skill set.
- Training isn't something you do once and it's over. Training is a process, like learning, that continues every day and changes to account for the dynamic, changing interactions between dog and human.
- The goal of training isn't to create a robot dog who rigidly follows commands. Training provides dogs with a large toolbox of skills, understandings, and communication techniques that allow them to calmly navigate their surroundings with independence, confidence, and flexibility.
- Don't underestimate how challenging it is to train a dog well. Some dogs struggle more than others to adapt to life in a human environment, so be patient, consistent, and persistent. And enjoy the challenge, since ultimately it will be a win-win for all.
- Since one goal of training is to build a relationship with your dog that strengthens the bond between you, don't outsource training. If you need help, hire experts who are officially certified

to practice dog training, but remain closely involved. Choose your dog trainer as carefully as you would a neurosurgeon.

- Positive or "soft" training techniques are more successful and more humane than fear- or punishment-based techniques. There is never any reason to hurt or scare a dog.

Smell

We begin with the sense of smell, which plays the lead role in a dog's experiential world. A dog's world is a continuous cacophony and symphony of odors swirling around and into their noses. As "nosed animals," a term we borrow from Alexandra Horowitz, dogs live in, and are consumed by, a world of smells.[1] Our human sensory experience is dominated by sight, so to understand the world from our dog's perspective, we really need to use our imagination and think about "seeing" the world through our nose. When we walk dogs on a leash and they stop to smell something, it is almost like they are stopping to read a very interesting news headline or hear some important neighborhood gossip. Dogs gather information first and foremost through their nose, not primarily through their eyes or ears.

And it seems like dogs are *always* gathering olfactory information, not just when they have their noses obviously pinned to the ground tracking a scent, but even when they're just standing around looking like they aren't doing much of anything. The nose never stops. On a walk through the neighborhood, a dog is collecting all kinds of important information from sniffing: They learn about the other dogs who have previously been there, and how recently; they might learn about female receptivity and even perhaps what the other dogs were feeling. Dogs might also be sniffing while they are asleep; their noses never go to bed.[2]

The dog's nose is an amazing adaptation. In fact, the canine nose is a virtual work of art, like many other organs that evolve via natural selection. The noses of many breeds of dogs are much bigger than human noses, and the dog's olfactory center in the brain is proportionately larger than that of humans; this means that more of the dog's brain is dedicated to processing olfactory information. Dogs have 125 to 300 million olfactory receptors compared to our measly 6 million. On average, their sense of smell is about a thousand times more sensitive than ours.[3] They can track many smells at the same time, and they sniff approximately five times a second. Alexandra Horowitz has suggested that if we were to spread out a dog's nasal epithelium (the lining of a dog's nose), it would cover their entire body, while ours would only cover a mole on our shoulder.[4]

A dog's nose sends incoming air into two separate paths, one for breathing and one for smelling. (Humans have no choice but to smell and breathe through the same pathway.) Unless dogs are panting, they breathe in through the nose, not through the mouth.

Each dog is different, and their sensory experiences and needs may vary. A dog's breed or breed characteristics don't necessarily determine what will make the dog optimally happy, but it's worth thinking about the shape of your dog's nose and what gets them sniffing and snorting. Hound dogs such as English pointers and bassets are highly motivated by smells, and the opportunity to explore the world with their nose may be an even higher priority for them than for individuals of brachycephalic breeds, like pugs and bulldogs, who have short skulls with compressed noses. Like humans, short-nosed dogs tend to spend more time breathing through their mouths, so they likely take in and process less olfactory information than their longer-nosed compatriots. Dogs with very foreshortened snouts can also suffer from obstructed breathing caused by congenital defects, such as collapsed nostrils, which makes smelling more difficult. Because short-nosed dogs can't make full use of their olfactory sense, we need to try extra hard to enhance their world of smells and to offset their deprivation in this sensory realm with extra attention to other senses, such as taste and touch.[5]

Lots of people wonder whether dogs sense the passage of time. Do they know the difference, for example, when their human companions have been gone from the house for five minutes or five hours? Scientists don't have a clear answer to this question, but one interesting clue comes from the nose. Horowitz suggests that dogs are sensitive to changes in the strength of odors that are evaporating. Smells degrade over time and odors will grow fainter. So, for a dog, how faint a smell has become may indicate how much time has elapsed since the odor was in full bloom.[6] Dogs understand the scent landscape in very complex ways and can distinguish between newer and older scent trails. They can track scents that are up to a week old. How refined or well-developed this method of sensing time is awaits further study.

LET DOGS SNIFF!

Off-leash dogs spend about a third of their time sniffing.[7] On-leash dogs aren't typically allowed to sniff for nearly this long. How often have you seen someone angrily tugging on the leash, trying to make their dog "keep up" on a walk? This is a form of sensory deprivation. In a *Whole Dog Journal* story about leash-walking behavior, the author's casual observation was that around 85 percent of the time dogs were pulling or dragging their humans down the street or vice versa.[8] Sometimes a dog wants to surge forward and get somewhere more quickly than the owner; sometimes a dog stops to intently investigate some smell and their impatient companion is the one tugging the lead, saying, "Come on! Let's go! I'm in a hurry." Or, "What are you doing? There's nothing there!" This second remark indicates a lack of knowledge about what dogs are sensing — we may not see anything of interest, but our dog certainly smells something fascinating. These complaints also embody a typical mismatch between our expectations and desires on a walk and those of our dog. Dogs aren't in a hurry to pee and poop and go back inside. After all, for many dogs, the daily walk (if they are lucky enough to get one) is their only time to really be out in the world and engage with it.

One easy way to enhance your dog's freedom is to accommodate their need to smell. When they are outside, whether on a walk or not, allow them ample time to exercise their nose and sniff to their nostrils' and brain's content. This is one of the simplest enhancements we can provide. *Let them sniff!* If there are places where your dog can be off leash, by all means give them this opportunity to walk or run at will, following their own olfactory agenda. When walking with a dog on leash, as much as possible let your dog set the pace. If your dog wants to linger over a bush, a clump of grass, or a fire hydrant, let them. Remember, some of the things that we might consider unsavory, like poop or pee, are very interesting to our dogs. Let dogs smell whatever they want, even if it seems disgusting; pee and poop are especially important because they contain a great deal of canine-relevant information.

Indeed, regardless of the apparent reason, when a dog resists our prodding and insists on sniffing, they're clearly telling us they've found something highly salient to them. In the context of animal behavior, the "salience" of a stimulus is the extent to which it stands out among other stimuli; the more salient, the more prominent or important the stimulus.

THE IMPORTANCE OF PEE-MAIL

For dogs, peeing is like leaving Post-it Notes around the neighborhood for other dogs to read, and sniffing pee spots is like reading the notes left behind by other dogs. Dogs like to smell the urine of other dogs, and they like to pee on all sorts of things, including on top of the urine of other dogs. This is called overmarking, and dogs may do it to cover up the scent of other dogs or to highlight their own scent. Urine is an extremely important tool that allows dogs to talk with one another about who was there and when, who's in heat, and perhaps how they are feeling. It's also possible that dogs recognize one another via urine, but research confirming this is not yet available. This is another reason not to expect your dog to pee once and be done. When dogs pee a little bit here, there, and everywhere, they aren't being indecisive; they might be leaving messages.

It was long believed that dogs marked their own territory when they peed, so that peeing on something meant: "This is mine; this is my turf. Be aware and stay out." However, we've learned that peeing has a much broader set of meanings for dogs. Some urinating may be territorial, but much of it is not. Sometimes dogs pee because they want to mask the odor of another dog's urine or be sure their scent is the one that others detect. And of course, sometimes dogs pee simply because they need to go.

We also know that dogs find the urine of other dogs more interesting than their own urine, and they will spend more time investigating a urine spot made by another dog than urine they left themselves.[9] Dogs often get so into sniffing urine it's impossible to get their attention; even a tasty treat won't work. Marc's dog Jethro earned the nickname Hoover because of his tendency to vacuum up the whiff of potent pee.

Dogs and their wild relatives will occasionally lift a leg without depositing any noticeable urine. This is called "dry marking." It isn't clear exactly why dogs dry mark, but Marc has hypothesized that leg lifting might be a visual signal that tells other dogs that pee was deposited, even when it wasn't. In this way, pee can be saved for when it is most needed. It's not uncommon to see dry marking followed by leg lifting and peeing within a few seconds, so in fact, the dog is not out of urine. Marc and his students showed that dogs dry mark more often when there are other dogs around who can see them, indicating this might be a visual display.[10]

Dogs also often scratch the ground after peeing or pooping. Dogs have scent glands in their paws, and when they scratch, they might be trying to send an olfactory message to other dogs by spreading the scent from their paws or by sharing the odor of the pee or poop they deposited. Scratching also leaves a visual mark on the ground. Ground scratching could be yet another form of social communication, and taken together, peeing, pooping, and ground scratching are a good example of how dogs may use composite signals to enhance their messages to other dogs, by using both olfactory and visual components. In other words, let your dog finish their message — give them time to scratch after they have peed or pooped — before continuing your walk.

LET 'EM ROLL

As offensive as it may be to us, the prospect of rolling on a pile of freshly mowed grass, a half-dried fish carcass, cow or elk feces, or some other nasty thing is very appealing to a dog. This is part of their natural behavioral repertoire and something their wild relatives also do.

Why do dogs roll in stinky stuff? We really don't know. They may be masking their own odor, or they may be making a statement about themselves by parading around with a strong or different odor. Whatever the reason, this is a behavior that dogs are motivated to perform, so we should let them do it, at least occasionally. Of course, this is one behavior that might need to be constrained at times, since most of us will want our smelly friends to have a good warm bath before re-entering the house, and we may not have time (and excessive bathing is hard on dogs' skin). Since your dog likely won't associate rolling in stink with the inevitable bath that follows at home, don't expect the bath to serve as a lesson for the future.

PROTECT THEIR SCENT IDENTITY: AVOID DOG PERFUMES AND DEODORANTS

An advertisement for Petco reads, "Keep your pup smelling delicious between baths with Petco's selection of dog perfumes, colognes, and deodorant sprays." But Jessica's dog Bella would be the first to tell you that she really doesn't like to smell like cherry or tea tree. She would much rather smell like Bella. A dog's scent is their identity. We may not be aware of our own odor, but dogs are most certainly tuned in to their own scent profile (and to ours). So, in the spirit of allowing dogs to be dogs, let your dog smell like a dog.

Groomers often use heavily scented shampoos and conditioners to make a dog smell "nice," which means that they carry or exude an odor that *we* like. Nobody really knows whether these strong artificial smells are aversive to dogs, but it's likely, given the sensitivity of dogs' noses. Odors are powerful triggers for people, and we aren't remotely as smell-oriented as dogs.

Because dogs communicate with one another through odor, changing their smell by washing it off or covering it up with perfumes will likely make communication with other dogs more challenging.

One very important thing to consider in trying to create

a comfortable home environment for our dogs is to think broadly about odors. We might find comfort in scented sheets, whereas dogs likely prefer bedding that smells familiar and doggy. When we leave dogs alone for the day, they might be comforted to be surrounded by odors that relax them, which means their own doggy odors and those of their favorite humans or of other pets in the home.

This is something to remember when or if you move to a new home, take a dog on vacation, leave your dog at home with a friendly dog-sitter, or take your dog to their favorite canine B&B (when they can't join you on a trip): Bring along a favorite dirty pillow or stinky stuffed toy — something with odors that will be familiar — to help your dog feel more at ease and less anxious.

AVOID OLFACTORY OVERLOAD

Because of their olfactory sensitivity, it's reasonable to ask if dogs can overdose on too many odors coming in at the same time or one after another. We know that dogs find all sorts of smells stimulating, but can they overindulge and suffer from too much of a good thing?

While it may be hard to imagine, dogs can suffer from sensory overstimulation that compromises their well-being. Being exposed to a strong odor for an extended period or being continuously bombarded with the same odor may lead to a feeling of sensory overload. Dogs, when their noses are full of a strong smell, may also be unable to recognize other odors that may be important to them. These may be odors signaling danger or telling them that a none-too-friendly dog is around. When there's too much background noise, we can't hear other people talk and we can't hear ourselves think.

Strong smells may be like irritating background noise to our dogs.

As of now, there has been no research into whether dogs find strong odors aversive or whether odors can compromise their well-being. But it is worth thinking about. Powerful body perfumes, strong disinfectants, heavily scented candles, or spray air fresheners might essentially be nasal assaults on our dogs (and often, when overdone, on humans as well). Does this mean that you should never wear perfume or cologne if you live with a dog? Never burn incense? Never douse the dog bed with Febreze? No, it doesn't, but your dog will likely appreciate it if you show restraint, and it might be a good idea to skip the Febreze. Dogs are already awash in artificial scents, from the laundry detergent we use to the formaldehyde in our carpets and furniture to the mint in our toothpaste. Dogs trying to live in a human-dominated world have their senses assaulted every second of the day, and we can help by giving them a break from too many strong, artificial scents.

People who work with dogs are already thinking about these things. For example, aware that the strong smells of chlorine and other disinfectants are aversive to many dogs, veterinary clinics (following the "fear free" model developed by Dr. Marty Becker) are using cleaners, such as hydrogen peroxide, that don't have a strong chemical odor. These cleaners are also designed to reduce the fear pheromones left behind by other dogs who have visited the clinic.[11] Some veterinarians, trainers, shelters, and researchers are also experimenting with aromas that dogs find calming, such as lavender.[12]

BUTTS: A CRITICAL CANINE COMMUNICATION CENTER

One behavior in which many dogs love to engage is butt sniffing. It may be mysterious to us — the siren call of the anal area — but this is undoubtedly a strong motivator for our dogs. To us, all dog butts may look (and smell) pretty much the same, but to our dogs, certain hind ends create a special buzz and require closer inspection.

Why is butt sniffing important for dogs? We really don't know much from formal studies, but it's likely that dogs gain information about individual identity — Joey smells like this, Lela smells like that. It's also possible they gather information about gender or about the reproductive state of the dog they're sniffing. While a dog's nose is traveling around the butt region, they're also picking up information from the anal glands that might tell them something about the other dog's emotional state, such as whether they're afraid or stressed out. All in all, though we find it rather uncomfortable and awkward, the entire anal area is a critical canine communication center, and we need to honor this doggy fact.

Human groins also are a part of the dog's olfactory landscape. We all know that dogs have a tendency to stick their noses into human groins, much to our own embarrassment. Groining dogs are not perverts; they're detectives. A human's groin is a cocktail of interesting and information-rich odors. From a dog's perspective, sticking a nose into someone's groin is not rude; rather, it's a normal part of saying hello, gathering information, and exchanging pleasantries. While we can teach our dog not to do this to strangers, we also shouldn't get our knickers into a knot if and when they do.

BURPS, GAS, AND DOGGY BREATH

We often laugh when a dog burps, but other than the sound effect, burps are not usually all that offensive. On some occasions, burps might serve a social function. Marc's friend Marije terEllen tells him that Benson, a five-year-old Bernese mountain dog, likes to come up to her, face-to-face, look her in the eyes, and burp. He seems to get a kick out of doing it, and he doesn't burp at other times. Is this his way of saying "hello" or "I love you"? Or is he just poking fun at his human? Marije insists that Benson is not mimicking her or her daughter, Arianne.

Like burps, farts are normal. Some people think dogs like to fart, but this isn't really known and there's no reason to think so, or not any more than we do. Some find dog farts gross, and some use dogs as scapegoats for their own indiscretions, but the bottom line is that all dogs fart. Sometimes a dog will seem surprised when passing gas or will "admit" to a fart, such as by turning around and looking curiously at their own butt or perhaps by leaving the room. Usually, dogs simply proceed as if nothing happened. And that's what we should do, too. A dog shouldn't be punished for farting, such as by scolding and banishing the dog to the backyard. This won't be understood by the dog and will seem arbitrary.

That said, excessive flatulence or burping can also be a sign of a serious medical problem and isn't a laughing matter. Know what's normal for your dog and what isn't. Farting is often a sign of gastrointestinal upset: It may indicate that a change in diet or a certain food isn't agreeing with the dog's stomach; it might indicate a GI illness, such as inflammatory bowel disease, or food allergies. As dogs age, they often become more flatulent because they begin to lose muscle tone and control in their sphincter (something that also happens to people as they age). Jessica's fifteen-year-old dog Maya is pretty much constantly farting, and Jessica can always tell what room Maya is in just by smell.

Dog breath is another source of amusing complaints for us, and as if in on the joke, dogs seem to love to get up close and personal and breathe right into our faces. Generally, adult dogs have worse breath than puppies; the somewhat distinct and sweet smell of "puppy breath" is related to a lack of bacteria in the mouth. When adult teeth start coming in, the lovely scent of puppy breath disappears and is replaced by plain old dog breath. Some level of bad breath is normal for a dog, but particularly smelly breath is another warning sign that something might be wrong. Tooth decay, gingivitis, infected teeth, and other serious medical conditions can lead to bad breath. If you notice a change in your dog's breath, and if it smells especially foul, your dog should be checked out by a veterinarian.

One of the biggest favors you can do for your dog is to take care of his or her teeth by creating a habit (at least weekly) of tooth brushing. Few dogs enjoy having their teeth brushed, but if you start when a dog is a puppy and make the experience fun, it helps establish a routine. Flavored toothpastes and lots of treats and praise can help make the brushing experience a positive one. Your dog can enjoy a healthy set of teeth and gums, and you will be rewarded with reasonably tolerable dog breath.

Taste

A dog's sense of taste is far less sensitive than our own. Dogs only have around 1,700 taste buds, whereas we have about 9,000. Humans can taste all five flavors: salty, sweet, sour, bitter, and umami (savory). Dogs (as far as we know) taste only salty, sweet, sour, and bitter. It's interesting to note how much variation there is in how well and what sorts of things animals can taste. For example, pigs have a more sensitive sense of taste than we do, possessing about 14,000 taste buds. Chickens have only about 30 taste buds, while cats have around 470. During their evolution, cats lost the gene that detects sweet flavors.

Taste is an evolutionary adaptation for assessing whether something is edible, although the definition of "edible" clearly varies between dogs and humans. If you've ever watched dogs eat, you may wonder whether they taste anything at all as they vacuum down snacks and meals, chomping and spraying food far and wide. Although the table or bowl manners of many dogs are appalling by human standards of etiquette, they certainly enjoy what makes it into their mouths.

Dogs show remarkable variability in their tastes for different foods. Jessica's two dogs, Bella and Maya, are nothing alike. Bella has a wide palate and will eat carrots, peas, apples, raspberries, and nearly every other food offered to her. Maya dislikes fruits and vegetables and will carefully pick them out of Jessica's offerings, even if they're hidden under thick gravy. Marc's dog Jethro was the consummate omnivore, refusing just about nothing: He ate everything he was offered or that he discovered on the floor, on a counter, or outdoors while on the prowl. One of his nicknames was Leadbelly. On the other hand, Marc's dog Inuk was a disturbingly picky eater who would stick his nose up even when offered a patty of wet dog food laced with ketchup — something Jethro would instantaneously inhale without a snort. Variety is the spice of life. Indeed, dogs may enjoy, as we do, experiencing a variety of taste sensations. Who wants to eat the same stuff every day? That's boring.

LET THEM EAT PASTA

Dog advice columns often decry giving dogs "people food," but there is no scientific evidence that the foods we eat are necessarily bad for dogs — or at least, no more bad for them than they sometimes are for us. Indeed, this distinction between people food and dog food is more of a marketing gimmick than anything else. Dogs coevolved with humans in part by eating our leftovers and throwaways. Claims that foods such as bread and pasta are bad for dogs don't have any scientific backing. Setting aside food that is unhealthy for anyone or poisonous, most of the foods we eat seem acceptable for dogs to eat (however, see the list of cautionary foods below). Further, it's downright absurd to throw away leftover meat from our own dinners and then open a can of "chunk of beef" for a dog's nightly meal. This not only wastes food but is probably less healthy for the dog. Like all processed foods, canned dog food is usually of inferior quality and probably not nearly as satisfying as fresh or freshly cooked steak will be.[1]

When it comes to diet, some people often compare dogs with their wolf ancestors. Advertisements for dog food may tout something along the lines of "Feed the wolf in your dog" or "Dogs evolved, but their instincts remain." One of Maya's favorite treats is called My Little Wolf (Turkey Bliss flavor). However cute as advertising, these sorts of comparisons can be fraught with error when it comes to actual feeding advice. For one, very few modern dogs exercise or engage in wolf-like behavior patterns and activities, which require a high-caloric intake. In addition, dogs and wolves may no longer have identical nutritional needs. For example, researchers recently uncovered an interesting genetic difference between dogs and wolves, namely, that dogs appear to have a greater ability to digest starches. The wolf genome has only two copies of the gene alpha-amylase 2B (AMY2B), which helps with the processing of starch in the pancreas, while dogs have somewhere between four and thirty copies of this gene.[2] When it comes to diet, treating dogs like wolves doesn't make biological or nutritional sense.

The truth is, there is still much we don't know about the ideal canine diet, despite the many claims we hear from dog food manufacturers, veterinarians, and self-proclaimed dog experts. Very few of these claims are backed by scientific research and actual evidence, so it's best to treat this advice as mostly opinion and anecdote, some of which is clearly intended to sell this or that brand of dog food. Further, what's most essential is to pay close attention to what your dog likes and dislikes and feed their fancy.

For instance, many veterinarians recommend sticking with the same food and never deviating, since some dogs get an upset stomach if their food is switched out. Although each dog owner needs to know their dog's gastrointestinal patterns, many dogs can happily enjoy a variety of different foods. Don't be afraid to experiment, and learn from your dog. At minimum, many dog food companies provide several flavors of dog food with the same basic nutritional profile, so even dogs with sensitive digestion can enjoy salmon one month and chicken the next, without much gastrointestinal drama.

Obviously, dogs don't read labels, and they will often eat things that are not good for them or that are dangerously poisonous. It's our responsibility to know what these foods are and to make sure that the foods our dogs eat are safe and healthy. Chocolate is a prime example, since it can be toxic to dogs in large quantities, and some dogs are sensitive even to small pieces that they may find lying around. Never leave a large dark-chocolate cake sitting on the counter if you have a counter-surfing dog! But there are less obvious trouble foods that we need to keep out of reach of our canine companions. If you are going to let your dog experiment and taste broadly — and you should — keep them away from foods and additives that can be harmful to them. These include chocolate, onions, garlic, avocados, nutmeg, grapes and raisins, macadamia nuts, caffeine, alcohol, marijuana, and xylitol, a sugar substitute that can be found in some sugar-free foods and gums. Finally, as we say, remember that unhealthy processed meats and sweets always make an unhealthy diet. A lunch of hot dogs, Ho Hos, and soda isn't healthy for us, and certainly not for our dogs.

TASTING TO HELP SMELL: A DOG'S "SECOND NOSE"

Dogs possess what some people refer to as a "second nose," called the vomeronasal organ (VNO) or Jacobson's organ. This structure has sensory neurons that detect chemicals and is used to enhance an odor by adding taste. The VNO is a group of cells within the main nasal chamber, and while the tongue is not part of the VNO, it is used to move chemicals into the VNO. So, for example, when Bella tastes the urine of other dogs, she's really getting an enhanced whiff accompanied by more information about who peed. The VNO is especially attuned to detect pheromones, chemicals that contain information important in social interactions.

Although humans send and receive chemical signals, we don't have a functional vomeronasal organ. But many other mammals do, and we can see it in action. For example, some ungulates, such as mountain sheep, taste the urine of females to see if they're in heat and ready to make more sheep, and when they do, they often curl their lips upward in what is called the flehmen response. Horses and cats also make this funny, lip-curling, teeth-baring face, but dogs typically do not display the complete flehmen response like other animals.[3] However, dogs engage their VNOs in other ways. Sometimes a dog's teeth will chatter after they lick urine or some other strongly scented area, and they may engage in what some call "tonguing," where the tongue is pressed rapidly and repeatedly against the roof of the mouth to help move chemicals into the VNO and thus help analyze a scent.

Dogs often put their tongues into substances or onto places we might find objectionable or embarrassing in human culture, such as when dogs lick another dog's pee. However, the tongue serves an important function in enhancing dogs' sensory experiences, and this is yet another situation where we need to put aside our own cultural hang-ups about what's "appropriate" and understand our dog's behavior within the context of canine culture.

EATING GROSS STUFF: TASTING THE WILD

A couple of years ago, when Jessica was walking Maya in the desert around Fruita, Colorado, Maya found a series of tasty discoveries: a deer femur, a dried-up cow patty, a mystery morsel disguised as trash, and a who-knows-how-old pork rib left behind by picnickers. Jessica's maternal instincts were in full swing, and she rushed after Maya, taking away one thing after another. Finally, Jessica's husband, Chris, said, "Why don't you just let Maya be a dog?"

Point well taken. One of the basic canine instincts is to search out and find food. And a dog's definition of food is not the same as ours. It extends well beyond grocery-store kibble. Further, the concepts of *edible*, *palatable*, and *nutritional* are not necessarily the same. Whether or not some of the nasty things that dogs decide to put in their mouths have nutritional value, we should let our dogs be dogs and taste the world around them if they wish.

Of course, we may sometimes have to set limits for our own welfare. Marc remembers when his dog Moses, a giant malamute, joyfully feasted on cow patties and ran up to Marc to proudly share the odor along with some chunks that were spewing from his mouth. Moses was having a ball, but Marc stopped him because they soon were going to share a car ride back to Boulder, and there would be no escaping the smell.

It won't surprise most people that veterinarians have specific terms for behaviors related to eating gross stuff. Perhaps the most distasteful to us is when dogs eat the excrement of other animals, a behavior known as *coprophagia* (from the Greek *phagein*, "to eat," and *copros*, "feces"). Maya particularly likes deer and elk poop, garnished with a little prairie dog poop, but goose poop is the pièce de résistance. It's not entirely clear why dogs eat poop. Veterinarian Ian Billinghurst, in his book *Give Your Dog a Bone*, describes poop eating as a natural part of the dogs' scavenger lifestyle. Dogs, he says, "receive valuable nutrients from material that we humans find totally repugnant. Things like vomit, faeces, and decaying flesh." He goes on to say that feces may be highly valuable foods for dogs because they contain so much bacteria, serving as a kind of natural probiotic and adding extra bacteria to the gut's microbiome.[4]

Some dogs also eat their own poop or the poop of other dogs. Puppies are more likely than adult dogs to eat their own poop, and they generally outgrow the habit. Further, dogs seem to prefer fresh stools.[5] For the most part, eating dog poop won't harm a dog, although worms and bacteria can be present in excrement.

Although it is a natural behavior, coprophagia can sometimes signal an underlying medical problem, such as gastrointestinal upset or inadequate absorption of nutrients by the gut. It should be discussed with a veterinarian, especially if it is a behavior that develops suddenly, if it is taken to an extreme, or if a dog clearly isn't feeling well after a meal of poop.

Since we don't really know why dogs eat poop, this is an area ripe for more research, but we understand why credible scientists, especially those worried about receiving tenure, might choose other areas of inquiry.

Nonfood objects also can make their way into a dog's mouth and then be swallowed, both accidentally and on purpose. One veterinarian friend recently recounted to Jessica a long list of strange things he'd surgically removed from dogs' stomachs, which included socks, wine corks, and a plastic Tyrannosaurus rex. Clearly, eating a foreign object can become life threatening for a dog (and expensive for an owner), since a dog can choke on the object, the intestinal tract can get blocked, or the object can tear the esophagus, intestines, or stomach.

For example, some dogs will remove the plastic squeakers from inside toys and swallow them. One morning last summer, a puppy friend of Jessica's named Poppy was happily chewing on a squeaker toy. Poppy's human looked over and saw that Poppy had dissected the toy and removed the squeaker. Just as her human reached out to take the squeaker away, the squeaker disappeared down Poppy's throat. Poppy had to have the plastic squeaker surgically removed from her stomach. She now lives in a squeaker-free home.

"Depraved appetite" (also called pica) is a behavior in which a dog eats dirt, stones, wood, or other nonfood objects. Although not entirely understood by scientists, one possible explanation for pica is that dogs may have a nutritional deficiency (such as in iron levels). Pica may also have a psychological component and could be a response to stress. Humans, particularly young children, can also suffer from pica.

Clearly, we shouldn't let our dogs eat anything and everything. We always need to pay attention to what dogs put in their mouths because sometimes they don't have good sense about what they should swallow. For example, the pork rib Maya found in Fruita was a bad idea, since cooked bones can splinter and cause damage to a dog's stomach or intestines. Veterinarians disagree about the safety of raw bones. Although some say that raw bones are a healthy way to satisfy a dog's desire to chew, some worry about possible damage to the teeth and about E. coli and other harmful bacteria that can be present on raw bones or in raw meat–based foods.

As responsible guardians, we have an impulse to protect our dogs from all dangers they may encounter. This is well intentioned, but we need to make sure we are being reasonable in what we ask of our dogs. Use your good judgment and stop them from eating things you know will make them sick or cause them harm, but just don't overdo it.

ALWAYS PROVIDE FRESH WATER

Like all mammals, dogs have taste receptors for salty, sweet, bitter, and sour. As far as we know, they don't have receptors for the so-called "fifth taste" of umami, which is often described as savory or meaty and which appears to be linked to taste receptors that respond to an amino acid called glutamate. Dogs may also be different from us in having the ability to taste water. Water is more salient to animals than we might have assumed, and the mammalian brain may possess specialized nerve cells that sense water (insects and amphibians have these nerve cells). Some researchers have even suggested that water is a sixth taste.[6] Although not all scientists agree, some have argued that dogs do, indeed, have taste receptors for water. These receptors are located on the tip of the tongue, which dogs curl to lap water. This area of taste buds on the tongue appears to be extra sensitive after a dog has eaten salty or sugary food. Dog psychologist Stanley Coren suggests that the ability to taste water "evolved as a way for the body to keep internal fluids in balance after the animal has eaten things that will either result in more urine being passed, or will require more water to adequately process."[7]

Can dogs also smell water? Anecdotal evidence from dog owners suggests that maybe they can, and this citizen science can help generate more formal research into the sensory world of dogs. For example, in early January 2017, Marc was sitting outside of a coffee shop in Boulder when he made friends with a handsome bloodhound who happened to be walking by. After receiving permission from Tommy's human, Marc rubbed Tommy's shoulders as they talked about Tommy's lovely disposition, his beautiful long ears, and his amazing nose. Then Tommy started pulling toward a water bowl he couldn't have possibly seen. Tommy's human casually remarked, "He can smell water." Marc was astounded, as he had never thought about this possibility.

While research continues into whether dogs taste or smell water, one important fact is well established: Dogs like fresh cool water better than warm stale water that's been sitting in the bowl for days on end. This may provide a simple explanation for the seemingly universal desire of all dogs to drink from the toilet. Since toilet water has likely been refreshed more recently than the water in Fido's bowl, it tastes better. Although unlikely to cause major problems, toilets can have residues from cleaning products and can harbor bacteria. If you live with a dog, redirect your dog's attention to their water bowl by making sure the water is fresher and tastier than the toilet water.

All water isn't the same to all dogs. It's important to learn what your dog likes and dislikes. Some dogs are not very discriminating about their water, whereas others have more refined tastes and won't drink from a "public" bowl. Maya, for example, won't touch water that has been "polluted" by another dog, such as the water bowl at the dog park or outside the coffee shop, no matter how thirsty she is. So, when taking Maya for a hike or out on errands, Jessica must make sure to pack clean water and a bowl for Maya. On the other hand, Jerome, a dog Marc knew at a local dog park, loved "the filthiest water he could find," according to Jerome's human, and yet, apparently, Jerome never got ill.

While it may be obvious advice, it's amazing how easy it is to forget the obvious in the hustle-bustle of a day. Do your dog a big favor and make sure they always have access to fresh water. Wash your dog's water bowl every day, and refresh the water several times a day, if you can. This is a simple way to enhance your dog's life. We know from our own experience that there's nothing more satisfying than a fresh, cool glass of water.

Why clean the water bowl daily? First, because putting clean water into a rank bowl does not provide clean water for your dog, since the water is immediately dirtied. Second, the reason a dog's water bowl gets dirty so quickly is because of the way dogs drink. Dogs don't sip water like a person but stick their tongue into the water and create a little scoop by pulling the tongue backward and up. Watch a slow-motion video of dogs drinking — it will likely surprise you.[8] The mechanics of how dogs lap water explains why there is so much drool and slobber and mess when they drink, and this introduces a lot of bacteria into the water. And what provides a nice, friendly environment for bacteria to grow? Why, tepid standing water.

This is why your dog will be happier if the water bowl is cleaned daily with soap and hot water and refilled regularly with cool water.

LET THE DROOL FLY

Something all dog owners know, but few of us love, is dog drool, aka slobber. In essence, *drool* and *slobber* simply refer to saliva that's no longer in the dog's mouth but rather is collecting on your pant leg, your cheek, or the floor under the dining room table. Saliva is perfectly normal, and so is drool. A dog's salivary glands are constantly producing and excreting saliva into the mouth, and this production increases when dogs smell or taste something enticing.[9] There's no way to avoid that.

Like human saliva, dog saliva helps with eating and digestion, and it's composed of water, mucus, electrolytes, and enzymes. Saliva binds food together into a kind of slippery bolus and lubricates the mouth and the esophagus so that the bolus of food can go down smoothly, without damaging the lining of the throat. Saliva helps make dry food soluble, and the enzymes in saliva break down starches, which is necessary to the digestive process. Perhaps counterintuitively, saliva also helps keep the mouth clean because it flushes away food debris.

Saliva production is related to taste and touch sensations in the mouth and on the tongue, and it is controlled by the brain, which explains why certain stimuli can increase saliva production, for example, when a very anxious dog salivates during a thunderstorm. Salivating also is a way for dogs to cool down (through evaporation of the liquid), and excessive salivating can indicate a problem with overheating.

Drooling is a reflex and not a behavior per se. Dogs can't help it. So don't get mad at your dog for prancing around with drool droplets hanging from their lips or for shaking their head and sending slobber flying all over the place. If you don't mind a little drool, but don't savor a drool shower, you might avoid certain breeds of dog, such as St. Bernards, mastiffs, bloodhounds, and Newfoundlands. Dogs of these breeds have loose upper lips, or "flews," and this anatomic abnormality causes them to drool a lot.

Of course, there's normal drool and there's extra-heavy drool, which might start dripping from a dog's jowls when watching someone chow down on delicious-smelling food. While we often laugh when dogs are drooling like Niagara

Falls, it's important to know that excessive drool, or hyper-salivation, can be a sign of a serious medical problem, such as periodontal disease, nausea, anxiety, oral or dental disease, or motion sickness. Drooling can also be caused by pain or injury in the mouth that keeps the dog from swallowing. *Ptyalism* is the fancy word that veterinarians use to refer to excessive drooling.

Are there solutions to drool? Yes, carry around a towel or bib to wipe the excess. But don't do anything drastic like buying "mouth diapers" or having surgery to reshape your dog's lips. Dogs should be free to drool normally. In fact, we can celebrate our dogs' special talents. November 16 is National Slobber Appreciation Day. Share your favorite drool pictures with other slobber lovers.

All in all, drooling is something all dogs do, and it's a waste of energy to get aggravated by it. Know what a "normal" level of drool is for your dog, and if your dog drools excessively, make an appointment with a veterinarian. Otherwise, accept and love your dog *and* their drool.

THE JOYS OF WORKING FOR FOOD

Sometimes people claim that they wish they could be a dog because they'd just get to lay around, sniff, drool, play, and have food delivered to them in a bowl. It may surprise you, then, to know that a life of laziness is not actually what dogs want or need. Research on a whole range of different animals shows that they'll choose to work for their food rather than take a "free lunch." This seems counterintuitive, but it's well established in the scientific literature. Studies conducted in the 1970s on pigeons, for example, found that they'll continue to peck at a key to get a food reward, even if the same food is available for free. Researchers sometimes call this phenomenon "contrafreeloading." Contrafreeloading behavior has been observed in many different species, including dogs, mice, rats, monkeys, and chimpanzees. The glaring exceptions within this research have been domestic cats, who seem to prefer being served by their human pet.

Anyone who's lived with more than one dog knows there are differences in how hard dogs will work for food. Trainers will often use the phrase "food motivated" to describe this propensity. Some dogs are willing to learn tricks or do other things to get food, whereas others want to be fed for just being alive and so darn cute. Clearly, there are individual differences in the canine work ethic, and one aspect of knowing your dog and providing the best life possible is to be aware of individual attitudes toward hard work. Some dogs are motivated to work hard because they're industrious. Others give up more easily; they are what we might call "lazy." However, avoid labels and judgments and simply respond to your dog's individual personality. If your dog really enjoys working for food, keep their life interesting by asking them to do some work and earn it.

Researchers have noted that there are two aspects of having to work for a reward like food. The first is called extrinsic motivation — the actual reward, the kibble or biscuit — and the second is intrinsic motivation, or the feeling of achievement individuals experience by having worked for that reward. Effort or work can be intrinsically rewarding because it can create positive feelings in animals and humans alike.

The reward centers in our brains are wired to offer pleasure in exchange for hard effort. Just as animals may find work or effort rewarding, they may find lack of meaningful work or activity to be stressful or boring.

Some positive stress, or what researchers call "eustress" (such as being asked to work for food), can be enriching, but it's important to know when good stress becomes harmful stress. Indeed, when too many demands are placed on an animal, whether these are demands for work or the demands of having nothing meaningful to do, animals can slip into psychological depression. For instance, dogs can suffer from "learned helplessness," which was first studied in detail by Martin Seligman and his colleagues at the University of Pennsylvania. Learned helplessness refers to situations in which animals get to a point where they learn that nothing they do can get them out of a specific situation, so they give up. One barbaric set of studies involved the use of inescapable shock. After dogs and other animals were trained to do something to get away from the shock, the experiment was changed, and no matter what the animals did, they couldn't avoid the shock. Another study put rats into a water tank with slippery sides and no means of escape. The rats would swim and swim and swim, but at some point, they would simply give up and drown.

Referred to as "behavioral despair" tests, these are one of the most common models for studying depression, even though they also are among the most inhumane and reprehensible types of research. However, what we now know about learned helplessness can be used to help us understand the stresses under which companion dogs live when they cannot remove themselves from bad situations. This can include chronic pain (for example, from arthritis); chronic boredom;[10] being continually chained; being exposed to things that are scary, such as constant loud noise; and physical punishments, such as being yanked on a leash.

Animals clearly need to have a sense of control over their own environment, and working for food offers some sense of control. In early studies of animal husbandry and welfare, farm and laboratory animals who were given control over aspects of their environment — such as food, water, and light, by being able to obtain these through pushing a lever — grew up to be more self-confident, more exploratory, and less anxious. In short, they were emotionally healthier than animals forced to live under similar husbandry conditions who were given no control over their environment.[11]

Most dogs like to eat, and having them work for their meals or treats is a good way to challenge them and to enrich their lives. However, just remember that *asking* a dog to work for food is not the same thing as *making* a dog work for food. Some dog trainers insist that a dog should never get "free food"; for each little bite of kibble, the dog must do a trick or something "good." If this works and the dog is clearly not overly stressed by having always to perform for food, this may be a reasonable approach. Be guided by your dog's well-being, not a need to control them. For instance, Marc's friend David used to ask his dog, Rusty, to spin around on his hind legs for food. Rusty clearly enjoyed doing this, but he did not *have* to do it for David's attention or to get food. If David asked him to spin and Rusty said no, he got fed anyway.

Food can be a very useful training tool. But your dog's life needs to be about more than obeying commands imposed by humans. There's nothing wrong with giving a dog a treat between meals just to be friendly. This is what we do among ourselves, and it's good for the dog and the human for the same reasons, since it helps to develop and maintain strong and positive social bonds.

Behavioral enrichments for bored dogs often center on food and feeding time. One way we can keep dogs entertained if we must be away from home for part of the day, or will be busy at the computer, is to get them something that takes a while to eat. Many different food puzzles are available at pet stores, and these can be great for dogs who like a challenge. They can also be very frustrating, so take the time to listen to your dog. Some ideas for homemade food challenges include popsicles made by freezing peanut butter or wet dog food in a Kong or small Tupperware or yogurt container, food-filled ice cubes, and frozen baby food. Search the internet for more ideas, and sometimes challenge your dog by hiding food and asking them to find it.

OFFER FOOD IN WAYS THAT SUIT YOUR DOG

What you feed your dog matters, but the ways in which food is offered are also important in developing and maintaining strong and enduring social bonds between you and your dog.

There's no simple rule about how dogs should be fed, and each dog needs to be treated as a unique individual. One of the things we can do, as human caretakers of our canine friends, is to pay attention to the vehicle that's used to give them food. It's important to think about your dog's shape, size, physical capabilities, and eating style in relation to the shape, size, placement, and height of the food bowl. What might work best to make eating pleasurable and easy for your dog? A few examples of frustrating situations for a dog might include a very hungry dog trying to eat kibble from a slick flat plate because the kibbles keep moving out of reach of their tongue; a basset hound who always comes away from dinner with half of the meal stuck to their ears; or a pug who must struggle to reach their nose down to the bottom of a very deep dish. For older dogs, a raised bowl can make eating more comfortable. Elevated food bowls are good for very large dogs — think about having to bend down to below your knees to eat your food — and shallow bowls are nice for puppies and short-nosed dogs.

Some dogs certainly "wolf down" their food, and some people like to brag about it. However, wild animals don't necessarily do this except under certain conditions. For dogs who eat too quickly or gulp their food, which can make them sick, a slow feeder might be a good idea. Feeding by hand can be good for puppies because it helps build attachment and can help avoid competition for food, if older, bigger dogs are also present. Using different feeding methods can also reduce competition between older dogs who prefer different feeding styles.

HELP YOUR DOG STAY FIT AND TRIM

Freedom from overfeeding may sound totally counterintuitive, but too much food is unhealthy, and poor health is a freedom inhibitor. Being overweight can have a whole range of negative health effects for dogs. It can cause inflammation, heart disease, arthritis, ligament and muscle injuries, breathing problems, and liver disease, all of which can compromise a dog's health just as they do ours. It can make it less enjoyable for dogs to walk, run, and play and can thus reduce the overall quality of life.

It's estimated that more than half of all dogs in the United States and the United Kingdom are overweight.[12] Veterinarians talk about the canine obesity crisis in the same dire terms that public health experts talk about the human obesity crisis. Many consider obesity to be one of the top welfare concerns for pets. It's no coincidence that dogs and people have grown fat together: We and our dogs eat a lot of junk food, we eat more than we need, and we don't get enough physical exercise. Overfeeding is a form of mistreatment, and it can have serious consequences. Jessica heard a story from her local shelter about a dog who was adopted and brought back three months later after having gained forty pounds. He had to become part of the foster program; he needed a temporary home where he could be given extra physical exercise and brought back to a healthy weight before being adopted by another family.

Like humans, dogs can be both overfed and undernourished at the same time. Plenty of doggy "junk food" is available, such as the Pup-Peroni, Snausages, and Pup Corn dog treats lining pet store shelves, smartly packaged to appeal to human consumers. As with humans, a little bit of junk food probably won't shorten your dog's lifespan, but no one should live on donuts alone.

Think about what you put in your dog's mouth just as

you would think about what you put in your child's mouth. Consider the nutritional profile of your dog's food, not just the price, since as a rule, you get what you pay for. A great deal of the so-called food on the market is garbage. That said, a wide range of moderately priced high-quality foods are available. Do research and talk with your veterinarian about your dog's specific nutritional needs, so you can find a food that provides appropriate nutrition and, of course, that your dog enjoys. Many pet stores will allow you to return food products if your dog doesn't like them, so you and your dog can experiment.

Finally, if you have a dog who is a little wide around the belly, measure his or her food and include snacks in your overall calorie calculations. "Eyeballing" a half cup of kibble is deceptively hard — try it and see how accurate or inaccurate you are. If you offer an overweight dog table scraps, feed less at mealtime or make the table scraps part of their meal. For dogs who are insatiable, splitting the allotted food for the day into several smaller meals can help keep them feeling more satisfied. For example, now that Maya is a senior citizen, she eats four small meals a day. She has a thyroid condition that makes her feel very hungry, and the time between meals seems very long to her. There is no rule about only feeding dogs once or twice a day. Just make sure to measure out the day's food carefully so that you don't feed more than is healthy.

Individual dogs obviously vary in what they need and how they process food. If you are feeding processed kibble or canned food, keep in mind that the feeding instructions on the back of a bag of dog food won't necessarily be exactly right for your dog. The "amount to feed" guidelines given by dog food manufacturers are generally bloated. Their goal, after all, is to sell more food.

Food and feeding also can be emotionally complicated. For example, the food your dog eats can affect his or her mood[13] and some dogs are stress eaters.[14] Furthermore, for many people and dogs, food is love. Humans use food and feeding to build trust and attachment with their dog. And dogs, for their part, are very skilled at tugging at our heart-strings, looking longingly at us as though they are truly starving to death, even if they just ate half an hour ago. It can feel cruel to deprive hungry dogs of what they really want — namely, more food! But we don't do dogs any favors by allowing them to become overweight. Because we control their diet, it is our responsibility to keep them at a healthy weight.

Finally, here are two interesting research tidbits about food and feeding. First, Labrador retrievers have a reputation for being food hogs. Apparently, there is a reason for this: Labs have a genetic mutation that makes them exceedingly hungry.[15] And second, if your dog isn't "weight compromised," you could add a little fat to their diet, and it might have a surprising side effect: When dogs eat more fat than protein, their sense of smell may improve.[16]

CHEWING IS IMPORTANT

Dogs don't chew only to eat. Dogs like and perhaps even need to chew. Puppies may chew to relieve pain from teething, and some dogs may chew or gnaw on a bone to clean their teeth or to entertain themselves.

Unfortunately, when dogs share our homes, some of their chewing behavior may be unwelcome. We may get rightfully upset when our dog mutilates the television remote, our new shoes, or our sunglasses.

Naturally, dogs may not be able to discriminate what they should or shouldn't chew. They may not be able to tell the difference between the stuffed dog toy bought specifically for them and the beloved stuffed teddy bear on a child's bed. It's best not to scold a dog for chewing on the wrong things. Simply redirect their behavior. Chewing, per se, is not "bad" behavior. It's a totally normal and natural part of a dog's repertoire. Just lock up the expensive shoes and put dangerous stuff out of reach. As with toddlers, adults are responsible for ensuring that dogs don't have access to things they shouldn't, and if a dog chews something forbidden, we should scold ourselves, not the dog.

That said, and as with other behaviors, excessive chewing can indicate a problem. For example, obsessive chewing can be a sign of mental distress. A dog may be trying to deal with boredom, anxiety, or loneliness. If dogs are left home alone for long periods or not provided with enough stimulation, it can lead to stress and depression (see "The Joys of Working for Food," above). When this is the case, it seems patently unfair to punish dogs for trying to adapt to these stressors through chewing, barking, digging, or some other "bad" behavior. Instead of punitive responses, dogs need our help. With chewing, we can often provide safe and appropriate alternatives to our couch, such as Kongs, bully sticks, or Nylabones. We should also seek to address sources of underlying emotional distress by making sure our dogs get ample attention, exercise, and stimulation.

Just as people disagree about the ideal diet for dogs, there's a considerable range of opinions about what makes an appropriate chew object for dogs. Many veterinarians advise against bones because they can break a dog's teeth. Some people think bully sticks are great; others worry that they may carry E. coli. Some swear by rawhide, whereas others consider rawhide a choking risk or worry about the safety of the chemicals used to treat the rawhide. The best advice we can offer is to get educated about the options and make a well-reasoned choice based on your dog's preferences, your budget, and what you consider a good balance between your dog's pleasure and their safety.

Touch

ouch, like the other senses, has many facets. In this chapter, we consider touch very broadly, so that it includes not just dogs' physical contact with the world but also their interactions with their physical environment and with other dogs and people.

Dogs touch the world, quite literally, when they walk, run, play, and sniff. Part of our exploration of touch, then, involves physical activity, such as going on walks, romping around a dog park, and riding in a car. Dogs touch noses when they say hello, they may touch nose-to-butt to gather information about one another, and they touch us when they rub against our legs or curl up next to us in bed. And, of course, we touch them when we pet, groom, and hug our canine friends.

We know less about the canine sensory experience of touch than we do about their sense of smell or taste. We know little, for example, about how dogs perceive human touch and why some dogs seem to like being touched while others don't. Does an aversion to touch develop during the socialization process, and what kinds of early experiences might lead dogs to feel uncomfortable rather than soothed by human touch? Why do some dogs simply seem to dislike human hands? In cases where a dog has an aversion to being touched, this needs to be honored, and we should always touch dogs on *their* terms, not ours. As with human-human touching, consent is important.

Touching often accompanies close encounters between and among dogs, and it's possible that it can add or detract from the messages that are being shared. We've seen a dog slowly walk over to a stressed dog, lie down next to her, and lay a paw over her back as if saying something like "all's well" or "I'm here, so relax." On occasion, dogs will groom one another, and often they sleep belly to back, feeling comfortable as they spoon. Touching can also lead to potentially explosive encounters, such as when, for example, one dog roughly puts his feet on the back of another and gets a quick and forceful rebuke. If you watch dogs playing at the park, you can see just how unique each dog is in how they touch other dogs, other people (friends and strangers), and their surroundings.

COLLARS AND LEASHES:
THE BALANCE BETWEEN CONTROL
AND FREEDOM

We mediate and control access to the physical and social worlds of our dogs quite a bit. We do this by deciding when, where, and for how long dogs get to be outside each day and, perhaps more subtly, by imposing the physical constraints of collars and leashes, which guide the speed and direction of a dog's movements. These tools of control are often necessary, but we should remain alert to the diverse ways in which they can inhibit a dog's freedoms and the ways these devices can themselves be harmful. Our goal should be to use these tools to facilitate access to a wide variety of positive physical and social experiences and to allow our dogs as much agency as possible.

Let's consider collars first, as they make direct contact with a dog's neck. Many different types are available, and the type of collar makes a difference to a dog. Flat collars are by far the most common. They are what most dogs wear around their necks with ID tags attached. Flat collars can be okay for walking with dogs who never pull and don't unexpectedly try to chase or bolt when on leash. But it is a rare dog who never jerks or pulls. A dog's neck is delicate and can be injured by violent jerks on a neck collar and even, presumably, by sustained hard pulling. Most of us have seen dogs straining so hard against their collar in their excitement to move forward that they can hardly breathe and sound a bit like Darth Vader. For this reason, more and more trainers and veterinarians are recommending that a dog be walked or run on a chest harness.

Choke collars and collars with sharp prongs, which are designed to make pulling painful, can also do serious damage if not used with extreme caution and under carefully controlled conditions. Many trainers advise against these types of collars altogether, in part because the risk of injury to dogs is significant. Contrary to popular belief, dogs don't have really thick skin on their necks, nor does their fur protect them from pressure on the neck. The San Francisco SPCA's website points out that the skin on a human's neck is ten to fifteen cells thick, whereas the skin on a dog's neck is only three to five cells thick. "So," they write, "if you think wearing a prong collar would hurt, imagine how your dog feels."[1] Along these lines, Dr. Zazie Todd, who runs the Companion Animal

Psychology website, notes, "We tend to think that since dogs have fur they must be more protected from these things than us with just our skin. But a dog's neck is a very sensitive area. If you think about the anatomy of the neck, it contains essential things like the windpipe. Applying pressure to the windpipe is not good for any dog, but can be especially serious in brachycephalic dogs that already struggle to breathe."[2] Prong and choke collars are typically placed on dogs with serious pulling issues. Many dogs will still pull, despite the discomfort, and are at risk of injury to their necks. Chest harnesses that clip in the front are thought to be a better choice for hard-pulling dogs, since dogs generally dislike the sensation of being pulled to one side.

Shock collars that allow a human to administer an electric shock to a dog's neck from a remote controller are widely considered problematic and are coming under increasing scrutiny by veterinarians, animal protection activists, and trainers. Especially as "e-collars" become increasingly cheaper and more available in pet stores and online, the concern is that dog owners will use these collars without sufficient background in dog training techniques or dog behavior, and so these collars will be used in ill-advised and harmful ways. In the hands of novice users, these collars are very bad news for dogs, though arguably, shock collars are bad news for dogs no matter what. In February 2018, Scotland announced a ban on the use of electric shock collars, citing concerns about the wide availability of these devices and the growing consensus that use of these collars is both ineffective and cruel.[3] Scotland joins a growing list of countries — which includes Germany, Norway, Sweden, Austria, Slovenia, Switzerland, Wales, and some states and territories in Australia — where the use of shock collars has been banned. We hope more will follow.

Collars and leashes are usually used together, since most collars can be attached to some sort of leash. One of the compromises dogs make to live in human environments centers on this tether, and to one degree or another, the leash will probably remain an enduring aspect of the human-canine relationship. In fact, leashes may have always been part of this relationship, though we may wistfully long for a previous time when dogs were allowed more freedom to run, and leash laws and ordinances were a thing of the future. In one of the earliest cave engravings depicting dogs, found by archaeologists in a sandstone cliff in the Arabian desert and likely dating back about eight thousand years, a hunter with thirteen dogs holds his bow drawn and ready. Two of the dogs in this engraved image have a thin line running from their neck to the waist of the hunter, representing what appear to be leashes and suggesting that humans trained hunting dogs much earlier than previously thought. Archaeologists aren't sure whether the thin lines depict an actual rope or leash or are merely symbolic of the bond between hunter and dog.[4]

Ultimately, a leash is simply a tool, a kind of umbilical cord between human and dog that can be used well or poorly. Used well, it gives dogs access to their world and can be a critically important freedom enhancer. Without leashes, dogs wouldn't be able to go many places with us. Used poorly, the leash can become a source of severe physical and sensory deprivation and harm. We need to be responsive to what's happening on both ends of the leash, and a walk should involve ongoing negotiations and mutual tolerance between dog and human. Leash pulling is certainly one of the most frequent points of contention between human and dog, and it may be one reason that many dogs don't get walked: It can become a real headache for someone to try to walk a dog who constantly tugs and pulls and strains. Walking on a leash is not a natural behavior for a dog, and indeed it goes against their natural instincts to run and explore. This is why we often need to devote considerable time and attention to training dogs how to walk nicely when on lead. This leash training is extremely important for puppies, but even adult dogs who haven't been properly schooled in polite leash walking can learn to accommodate their human. For their part, humans will be well rewarded for time spent helping their dog understand the how and why of leashes with many happy miles of walking together as a team.

WALKING THE DOG: ON EXERCISE, SHARED TIME, AND POWER STRUGGLES

For humans who live with dogs, walking is both good exercise and a good way to develop and maintain strong social bonds with their canine companion. Yet it can also become a power struggle with negative consequences for both.[5] When such a struggle ensues, it's usually the dog who gets the short end of the leash.

People often want to know how much physical and sensory exercise a dog needs each day, as if one could write a prescription: "Walk dog 30 minutes a day, morning and evening, x 7." While it's a good question, unfortunately there's no gold standard for how much walking a dog needs because this will be different for every dog and at every life stage. Puppies typically need a lot of play and exercise time, but they shouldn't be walked or run excessively, since their muscles, tendons, and bones are developing. Older dogs still need to stay active, and it's extremely important for them to get exercise that's appropriate for them. Of course, as they age, some dogs may need shorter and easier walks, with perhaps even more time for sniffing, and it's wrong-headed to assume that older dogs don't have much zest for life or don't need any walks.

Obviously, dogs need physical exercise, but there are limits. Yes, too much of a good thing can be harmful. We both live in Boulder County, an area with an extremely high census of superathletes. You can see their wiry, sweaty bodies rolling into the coffee shops on weekend mornings, just having completed a swim or a bike ride, followed by a ten- or fifteen-mile trail run with their dog. Dogs love to run, and some might enjoy a fifteen-mile run, but our canine companions want to make us happy and will often continue running or hiking well beyond what is comfortable for them. We need to set safe limits and pay close attention to what works for them. There's no shame if a dog balks at a long hike or run and simply wants to rest. If a dog with their behavior tells us, "Honey, not today. I'm tired," we should respect this request.

Notwithstanding the overexercised dogs of Boulder's superathletes, one generalization is safe: Most pet dogs don't get enough exercise and don't get to spend adequate time outside of their homes and yards exploring the world. A common figure thrown around by dog trainers is that an hour of exercise in the morning and an hour in the afternoon or evening is a good goal. Yet very few dogs are lucky to get this

much walking or running time. A recent survey of dog owners in the United Kingdom, for example, found that, on average every day, 20 percent of dogs are walked for an hour,
43 percent of dogs are walked for thirty-one to fifty-nine
minutes, 34 percent are walked for eleven to thirty minutes,
and 3 percent are walked ten minutes or less. These percent-
ages only refer to dogs who actually get walked. Believe it or
not, the survey found that about ninety-three thousand dogs
in Britain are never walked at all, ever.[6]

However, for many people, sharing your life with a dog
means taking some sort of daily walk, and this often becomes
a set routine: same time, same place, same route. That said,
despite this sense of routine, the walk itself can be many
things, and each day it can be something different. There's
always far more going on than simply snapping on a leash
and heading out the door. Sometimes we may treat the dog
walk as a necessary chore, and sometimes as a chance to get
some exercise ourselves. Sometimes we hurry our dog to do
their business quickly, and sometimes we let them linger.
Sometimes we may walk *with* our dog, treating the activity as
sacred time together and a chance to enjoy each other while
enjoying nature. Other times we may only walk *for* our dog,
letting our dog do whatever they want while we daydream,
send texts, talk to friends, and are mentally elsewhere.

How we view a dog walk may suggest certain things about
how we perceive our relationship with our dog. For instance,
consider for a moment these questions: Who is the walk for?
Is it for our daily exercise or the dog's? And what is the walk
for? Is it intended to get somewhere, to get out into nature, to
poop, to let the dog experience dogness by sniffing wherever

they choose? Whatever our perspective, the walk is an arena where the power relations between a dog and their human companion are negotiated. As an example, the tightness of a dog's leash during a walk may tell us something about that particular human-dog relationship in that moment. A slack leash may indicate that human and dog are walking in harmony, whereas a tight leash may suggest conflicting "agencies," that is, conflicting ideas about where the walk should go, how quickly they should be moving, and who is leading the way — in other words, who's controlling whom.

Thomas Fletcher and Louise Platt, two researchers working in the field of animal geography, have recently published an interesting study, "(Just) a Walk with the Dog? Animal Geographies and Negotiating Walking Spaces."[7] They suggest that a dog walk is far more than it first appears: It's a complex activity in which the personalities of both the dog walker and the dog are brought into play, and where the two are involved in a complex negotiation and even, at times, a power struggle. Walking, Fletcher and Platt write, is both an expression of the human-animal bond and a key activity through which that bond can be either strengthened or potentially weakened.

For their research, Fletcher and Platt conducted in-depth interviews with people in northern England who regularly walk dogs. Most of the dog walkers they interviewed felt a strong commitment to "listen" to their dogs, and they thought that the walk was an opportunity to allow dogs a degree of agency and freedom. Dogs were seen not as objects to be moved around by their owners but as agents and companions in the walk. The walk, including its timing, length, and location, was chosen based on what the respondents felt best suited the needs of the dog. Most of the respondents spoke of the walk as essential for their dog's health and well-being, and they believed that two walks a day of thirty minutes were sufficient. Although most respondents spoke of the walk as something they were obligated to provide as a part of responsible caregiving, they also viewed walking with their dog as something they wanted to do and enjoyed. As Fletcher and Platt note, this contrasts with the general tone of the literature on dog care, which tends to frame dog walking as an unpleasant chore.

Fletcher and Platt also found that people perceive their dogs to have subjective experiences, to feel emotions, and that the walk is about making dogs happy. "There was widespread belief," they write, "that dogs are happiest when out in the open, and it is here that they are able to best demonstrate their 'dogness.'" For example, dog owner Jane spoke about walking her dog, Copper:

> One of the biggest joys for us is when one of us stands at one part of the field and the other, and he just runs. And we've managed to time him. He does thirty miles an hour. And he looks like a cheetah, he looks like a wild animal. And it just makes your heart, I mean, I feel a physical change in my body when I watch him run, which has never been created by anything else, really.

Again and again in their interviews, Fletcher and Platt found people referring to the individual characteristics of their dog, listening to their dog's unique preferences, and expressing a commitment to making space for their animal's agency. This is the ideal we suggest striving for: Treat the walk as a way to help dogs be dogs within the constraints of human environments — to take them to wild places and to give them space to run, sniff, chase, roll, mark, and interact with other dogs and people (or not, as they prefer).

However, just as a walk can be a way for dog and human to share experiences and strengthen their bond, a walk can also be a time of anxiety, stress, power struggles, and unpleasant interaction. Stress can arise between dog and human, which can be expressed through what we might perceive as "bad behavior" on the part of the dog: lunging at other dogs or at people, barking and growling, acting distressed or obnoxious, pulling hard on the leash. When a walk becomes a power struggle, with the dog pulling one way and the human pulling the other, no one really enjoys the experience.

When this happens, our advice is to ease up on the leash and negotiate a peace settlement. Recognize that there may be conflicting agendas, and take some time to reflect on what you want from the walk versus what your dog, through their behavior, is telling you they want. When there is regular conflict, before you head out the door, try to adjust your goals and expectations so that the walk satisfies both of your needs as much as possible. This will help make sure that walking the dog strengthens your bond and gives you both the most enjoyment possible.

UNLEASH YOUR DOG: GIVE AMPLE OFF-LEASH TIME

While leashes can be a meaningful symbol of the human-canine connection — both tethered together, body and soul

— leashes are also, in their literal form, one of the most important constraints we place on our dogs' freedom. The leash restricts a dog's movement and reach, their pace and speed, to what their human prefers or demands. There are places we don't want dogs to go, things we don't want them to touch or bite, and places they shouldn't dig. The leash is also meant to restrict a dog's ability to engage in social interactions, whether with other dogs or people. We don't want to allow dogs free access to others when that encounter might be unwelcome, inconvenient, or otherwise undesired and unasked for.

Thus, off-leash time provides dogs with a rare opportunity — the freedom to explore the world at will, physically, mentally, and socially. We recommend trying to find places where your dog can run free every day on their own terms. If this isn't possible, make certain days *their* days and do your best to accommodate their needs.

A prerequisite of giving a dog off-leash time is adequate and appropriate training. Dogs need to know when and how to return to their human to be safely allowed off leash; in some cases, this is a legal requirement. Many of the hiking areas in Boulder County, for example, have "voice-and-sight" regulations: Your dog must come when you call and must always remain within your sight, or else you can be charged a fine and will be given a stern lecture by a ranger. The purpose of voice-and-sight regulations is to balance and accommodate the needs and well-being of everyone who shares the mountains: wildlife, Boulder residents, and other dogs. Despite the fantastic off-leash possibilities near Boulder, we see many dogs who are never unclipped. One of the most common things we both hear is, "Oh, Buddy would love to be able to run free, but I can't let him. He won't come back." A dog's freedom is directly related to how much time and energy their human is willing to devote to training. It's unfortunate when a dog is denied the opportunity to be off leash simply because their human is unwilling to dedicate this time.

That said, it's also the case that some dogs simply have difficulty with recall, no matter how much their human guardians work to improve their recall skills. Some dogs have a very strong prey drive, some have difficulty focusing attention, and some are just downright stubborn (often like their humans). For these dogs, a leash may always be necessary when out in the world. When this is the case, and in general, consider other options to allow off-leash freedom, as well as to increase a dog's range of choices and thus their own sense of self-determination. For instance, if you have a fenced yard, consider installing a dog door. This is a great enhancement that expands a dog's environmental milieu. They can choose to relieve themselves on their own schedule instead of having to wait to be let out, and they can be outside, breathe fresh air, and watch and listen for other animals.

Another opportunity for off-leash time, of course, is the dog park. Dog parks can be great places for dogs. Dogs can run free, interact with other dogs and humans, and play. Dog parks are the fastest-growing part of city parks.[8] In 2010, there were 569 off-leash dog parks in the hundred largest US cities, a 34 percent jump in five years, while overall parks increased only 3 percent.[9] Some dog parks also are making accommodations for special-needs individuals, and some cities are offering places for dogs and humans to interact that are in between homes and dog parks.[10]

Like so many other things, the appropriateness of a dog park depends on the dog, the park, the humans who frequent it, and all of these combined. Dog parks can be very stressful for some dogs, and each dog park develops its own personality, one defined by its particular population, much like human neighborhoods. Plus, some dogs find dog parks overstimulating or scary, so listen to your dog. Bella doesn't really like the dog park unless it is empty, in which case she enjoys sniffing here and there. Jethro loved dog parks and loved everyone he met there, human and nonhuman. Maya likes to go into the park, but there is one dog she dislikes in her neighborhood and who shares her feelings. They have come very close to getting in a fight, so Jessica doesn't take Maya into the park if "the enemy" is there. As with so many other topics, listen to and get to know your dog, and then honor their likes, dislikes, and choices.

Dogs are highly social, group-living animals, yet they're rarely allowed to engage in group activities (like play) that aren't contrived and controlled, since their social interactions are often constrained by leashes, fences, and humans. As such, it's difficult to know the importance of giving individual dogs the opportunity to interact with groups of other dogs, particularly groups that are stable over time.

At least at dog parks, dogs get to interact with groups of dogs, though often these are not stable groups, since on any given day, you don't know who will show up or if new dogs might arrive. Indeed, sometimes people are hesitant to allow their dog to romp and zoom around with dogs they don't know. However, dogs can learn lessons about social etiquette by interacting with strange dogs, just like we can. When these sorts of interactions aren't allowed, a dog might miss out on meeting some important behavioral needs. More research in this area would surely be of interest, and it could have important practical applications that could benefit dog-dog and dog-human relationships.

An example of research that bears on the social dynamics of groups of unleashed dogs is a study conducted by Zsuzza Ákos and her colleagues, who observed a group of six dogs belonging to the same household as they went on unleashed walks with their owner. The question the researchers wanted to explore was how a group of dogs decide the direction of their collective movements: Is there a leader, and how is this leader chosen, or is decision-making egalitarian? Researchers watched "leader-follower" relations and decision-making and tried to determine how each dog's position in a social hierarchy was based on developed social networks and personality differences in the dogs. These social interactions took place during off-leash walking, and the study would not have been possible, or would have been significantly influenced, by the presence of leashes. The researchers write, "Groups that are not able to coordinate their actions and cannot reach a consensus on important events, such as where to go, will destabilise, and individuals will lose the benefits of being part of a group."[11] Because leashes significantly impact group dynamics, further research involving groups of off-leash dogs (outside of dog parks) may help us better understand canine social dynamics.

Finally, we feel there is a desperate need for more research on the topics of leashes, off-leash time, and dog walking. We know that leashes influence dog-human and dog-dog social dynamics. But we don't know all that much about how and why. For instance, many people report that their otherwise amiable dog gets aggressive or unfriendly toward other dogs when on a leash. Several books have been written on what is called "leash reactivity," and leash reactivity has even become a category of behavioral diagnosis for dogs. But we don't have a good handle on why leashes trigger this behavior in some dogs and not others, nor about a whole range of other possible ways in which being tethered influences how dogs feel and how they behave.

NURTURE YOUR DOG'S FRIENDSHIPS

One reason dogs like to go to dog parks is to touch, see, and sniff friends or to meet other dogs who might become future friends. This is a wonderful enhancement we can offer them. One activity that dogs love is play. In addition to freedom, play requires two other important ingredients, namely, fun and friends. And dog parks are a good place for dogs to have all three. Dogs show preferences for certain individuals. Marc knew two dogs — Sadie, a small hairy mix of lots of different genes, and Roxy, a lean boxer mix — who were best friends. When Sadie arrived at the dog park, she immediately peed and then checked out who was there by lifting her head and sniffing, and then almost invariably she ran back to the entrance to wait for Roxy, who, if she was already at the dog park, raced up to Sadie around 95 percent of the time (according to Roxy and Sadie's humans). Then they would play as if they were the only two dogs in the world.

However, an interesting thing happened on the days when Roxy didn't show. Sadie would pace along the fence line and look around, clearly wondering where Roxy was, even as other dogs came up to say hello and ask her to play. Sadie usually paced for around twenty seconds or so, which is all the time she needed to establish that Roxy was absent. At that point, Sadie went off and found other dogs to play with.

How did Sadie know so quickly that Roxy wasn't there? We have no idea, but when Sadie chose to give up waiting and go find other friends with whom to romp, she was correct 99 percent of the time; Roxy wasn't coming. Is it safe to say that Sadie and Roxy were friends, and that they preferred to hang out and play together? Yes, it is, and their humans agreed. Using her senses, and perhaps even a sense of time, Sadie displayed an uncanny knack for identifying Roxy's presence or absence. And if Roxy was missing, did Sadie ever let her freedom in the dog park go to waste? Never. What dog would ever do that? She simply went off to find other dogs, familiar or unfamiliar, with whom to romp.

Playing with friends is a lot of fun because friends know one another's personality and play style and can jump right in without having to formally ask if they want to play or to negotiate the details. When old friends aren't present, dog parks allow dogs to make new friends and expand their social circle. A few years ago, Marc was thrilled when Alexandra Weber, an eighth grader at a Boulder middle school, emailed him to ask if he would help her with a science fair project on play in dogs. After enlisting her mother, Lisa, and her younger sister, Sophia, to become her field assistants, Alexandra and Marc decided to focus on the question of whether familiar dogs play differently than unfamiliar dogs. Alexandra thought that simple question had been studied extensively, but it hasn't. There are tidbits of ideas scattered about in the research, but no one has really studied this question in depth. Concerning this topic, dog trainer Patricia McConnell had previously written, "My observations suggest that dogs who are less familiar tend to play bow more to each other than familiar dogs do."[12] This might be because they must tell the unfamiliar dog what they want to do, since they don't know one another's style of playing and it could be risky to jump right in. However, we don't know if that really is so.

In Alexandra's study, which is an excellent example of citizen science, she used her two dogs — Tinkerbell, a highly social dog who loves to play with any dog, and Huggins, who is pickier about his playmates — as confederates in her study, which she conducted at a local dog park in Boulder. Alexandra discovered that play was more rough-and-tumble when familiar dogs played. When they knew the dog with whom they were playing, dogs weren't as worried about formalities, and they jumped right into play. All dogs in the study showed similar behavior. Overall, dogs who knew one another played more roughly and didn't take the time to sniff and greet one another. Dogs who didn't know one another were more formal and respectful. They took the time to get to know one another before starting to play by sniffing and nose bumping more than they did with familiar playmates.

Obviously, this question needs further research, but Marc was proud that Alexandra and her family became ethologists to help answer it, and her father also became much more interested in dogs. To top off her efforts, Alexandra won a science fair award for her research.

KNOW YOUR DOG'S PETTING PREFERENCES

You may not sit around thinking about what it means to have a pet dog. But the origin of the term *pet* captures something important about the human relationship to companion animals. The word *pet*, first recorded in 1508, is from the Middle English *pety*, meaning small. The term has been applied to both nonhuman animals and women and can mean (as a verb) "to stroke or pat affectionately" or (as a noun) "something one feels affection for" and "an animal kept in the domestic setting whose function is personal companionship or entertainment." Although the word may have insulting connotations, it also points to one of the positive components of our relationship with dogs: the physical touch that brings us together and forms the glue in the human-animal bond.

You don't have to be a scientist to know that many, if not most, dogs like to be petted. There is a scientific explanation for the positive role of touch in our human-animal friendships. The importance of touch has been well established for decades, beginning with Harry Harlow's famous (and famously horrifying) studies on infant rhesus monkeys. Monkeys who were raised on wire "mothers" suffered deep psychological trauma because of the lack of maternal touch. Touch is essential to normal mental and emotional development, not just for human babies but for all mammals (and perhaps other animals as well). Touch feels good. It can reduce blood pressure, lower cortisol levels, lower heart rate, and increase levels of oxytocin in humans and dogs alike.

Hairy-skinned mammals (which includes humans and dogs, among others) have a group of sensory neurons called C-tactile afferents. Gentle stroking of these neurons stimulates the release of oxytocin, often called the "love hormone" because it is associated with feelings of trust and affection in mammals. These neurons don't respond to rough touching, pinching, or poking. Petting feels good to both parties, the one who pets and the one being petted. What quality and quantity of touch feels good varies from one individual to the next, and different dogs have different thresholds for when and what kind of petting feels good and for when petting begins to feel invasive and uncomfortable.

Some dogs simply don't like being touched, while some don't like being touched by strangers or certain types of people. Such dogs are often labeled as "cranky," "mean," or "standoffish," but this isn't fair. These dogs may have good reasons for not liking to be touched, such as having had negative experiences with rough touching or physical punishment, or this may just be who they are. We should respect their desires, either way.

Sometimes dogs who have always enjoyed physical contact will withdraw. This can be because they're in pain and being touched doesn't feel good. It can also be a sign of anxiety or stress. A noticeable change in a dog's tolerance for touch should prompt a visit to the veterinarian to make sure everything is okay.

Touch should always happen on the dog's terms and with the dog's consent. We need to practice reading a dog's body language for cues about consent and about when, where, and how they want to be touched. For example, if a dog moves away from you or their body stiffens, this is a good sign they do not want to be touched. The better we understand the behavioral repertoire of dogs in general, and our own dog in particular, the more we will be able to respect their choices. To this end, closely observe some interactions between your dog and new people (and even make an ethogram) and watch for signals the dog gives about their interest in meeting and being touched by an unfamiliar person. What do you see happening to the tail, the ears, the eyes, the facial expression, and the position of the body?

The language of "personal space" is often used to teach children about respecting other people and to explain why it is rude and intrusive to touch other people or even get extremely close without first asking permission. *Personal space* is a term developed by anthropologists, and according to the English Oxford Living Dictionary, it is defined as the "physical space immediately surrounding someone, into which encroachment can feel threatening or uncomfortable." The study of personal space is called "proxemics," and researchers in this area have found that the amygdala is largely responsible for determining how much personal space an animal needs and why invasion of the space activates a fear response.[13] We can use the same basic principle to guide interactions with dogs: Don't touch without consent, and don't enter personal space without asking first. What constitutes "personal space" will vary from one dog to another.

It's worth noting that personal space is a two-way street, and dogs don't always respect our individual human boundaries.

For example, some people are uncomfortable when a dog (especially an unknown dog) jumps on them or rubs all over their legs, and at times dogs will ignore human signals. The human-animal bond can suffer when preferences related to personal space differ, such as when a very touchy-feely dog is adopted by a human who doesn't like touch, or when a standoffish dog is adopted by a human who wants constant physical contact. Keep this in mind when adopting a dog: Consider your own needs for personal space and those exhibited by the dog. Naturally, some give and take will always be necessary.

SIGNS OF AFFECTION: HUGGING AND LICKING

Our love for dogs often gets expressed in hugging, and dogs often return that affection by licking. These two intimate gestures translate our feelings of emotional closeness into physical closeness. Many dogs are hug magnets, and children seem particularly drawn to throw their arms around the furry neck or torso of a dog.

That said, as with petting, remember that some dogs find hugging uncomfortable, even frightening, and all dogs might have moments when they do not want to be hugged. Since hugging requires even more closeness than petting, an unexpected hug might make a dog nervous, and they may respond by snapping or even biting. Again, hugging is usually okay if it's done on the dog's terms, and the best advice is to err on the side of caution: When or if you're unsure, don't hug. As always, pay close attention to the personality of the dog. Understand their preferences and signals of consent.

Of course, dogs can't hug us in the same way, though they can certainly climb into our laps, lean in, and snuggle close. They also probably lick as a sign of affection, and being licked vigorously by a loving dog is a source of (sticky) joy. But here again, not all people like being licked, and dogs may not always lick to express emotion. It's also possible a dog will lick to use taste to get information about what we've recently eaten or who we've kissed.

WHISKERS ARE SENSATIONAL

Dog whiskers are undeniably cute, but they're not simply cosmetic. Whiskers, or vibrissae (from the Latin *vibrare*, "to vibrate") as they are technically known, are specialized hairs that help mammals interact with others and with their environment. Whiskers are different from pelage hair. Pelage is the hairy, woolly, or furry coat of a mammal, which serves its own important functions: It insulates, conceals, signals, and protects. Whiskers are longer, thicker, and stiffer, and they are exquisitely sensitive to touch. Each vibrissae follicle is distinctly represented in the sensory cortex of the brain, and each follicle has its own blood and nerve supply. In dogs and some other mammals, vibrissae are localized to the facial region, but some animals have vibrissae on other parts of their body, such as the forearms. Dogs have four sets of vibrissae: on their upper lips, their lower lips and chins, above the eyes, and on their cheeks. Take a moment right now to get a good look at your dog's whiskers and find the four different sets.

Vibrissae are an important part of the sensory apparatus for nearly all mammals, with the notable exception of the naked ape (that's us). Because we don't have whiskers, we may underestimate their importance to other mammals. These delicate sensory tools help wild mammals sense danger, find food, and navigate their environment, particularly during times of low light. Whiskers also pay a role in the social behavior of some species, such as rats. We don't know how whiskers function in the social lives of dogs, but it is likely that they play some role.

Research conducted in the 1970s on tactile sensation in rats, mice, and cats established the central role of whiskers. One classic study, for instance, involved removing the whiskers of rats and measuring performance in a maze test. Not surprisingly, rats deprived of whiskers had more difficulty completing a maze than rats with intact vibrissae. In fact, the deprivation of whiskers was found to be more significant than the deprivation of smell, hearing, or vision, which also makes clear just how cruel these vibrissae-removal experiments were. Although whiskers seem to be less critical to dogs than to rats, they're still an important part of a dog's sensory interaction with the world.

Dog groomers will often trim whiskers, if not specifically asked to leave them intact. Dogs used for show will often have their whiskers trimmed to achieve "clean lines" on the face, but the American Kennel Club discourages whisker trimming in most breeds. They recognize that whiskers serve important functions and, as in the case of the Pekingese, "add to the desired expression."[14] Because vibrissae are made of keratin, like pelagic (dense) hair, cutting them isn't physically painful to a dog, though plucking them is. Nonetheless, trimming the whiskers removes or blunts an important sensory modality for dogs. Hopefully, breed and grooming standards will continue to evolve to embrace the beauty and functionality of dog whiskers.

DOGS DIG TOGETHER TIME

By "together time," we mean the quality time that you and your dog spend together each day. Together time isn't just about petting your dog, but it refers more generally to all forms of social, emotional, and physical closeness. "Together time" is one of the most important enhancements in our book because what dogs most need from us is *us*, and that's the one thing many dogs don't get enough of. As with children, dogs enjoy new toys and special treats and a fancy new bed, but these aren't what they really care about. What they really crave is the company of their human companions.

Dogs are social animals, and they form strong attachments to their humans. Indeed, selection pressures on domestic dogs have favored the "hypersociability" gene. Dogs don't just tolerate human presence; they actively seek it out. It's safe to say that companion dogs *need* social closeness with humans, and deprivation of this social contact poses well-being concerns.

The UK government recently appointed a Minister of Loneliness to address the growing crisis of loneliness among the human population of the island nation.[15] We could very well also use a Minister of Loneliness for the pet dogs in the world. While Britain has data on the scope of its human loneliness problem — more than nine million people often or always feel lonely, according to studies done by the health ministry — we don't have good research on the problem of loneliness in companion dogs. But more and more veterinarians and trainers are starting to talk about canine welfare problems associated with social isolation and are connecting the dots between loneliness and growing numbers of behavioral and psychological disorders among pet dogs.

Millions of dogs are left home alone for long periods of time. Some are lucky enough to have access to the full house and a fenced yard through a dog door. Many others are locked in a kennel or basement or bathroom while their owner is gone, presumably to protect the house from destructive behaviors. A survey of UK dog owners found that more than a quarter of dog owners believe it is okay to leave a dog at home for over five hours a day.[16] Many dogs are stressed when left alone. Levels of cortisol in the blood increase, and they sometimes spike the entire time the dog is alone. Dogs may resort to obsessive barking or to destructive behaviors such as digging the carpet, chewing the couch, or destuffing all the pillows on the bed, the very behaviors that can lead owners to lock a dog in a kennel or garage, which further fuels a dog's anxiety.

How much alone time is okay for a dog? Nobody really knows, and surely it depends on the individual dog. Although behaviorists and veterinarians don't agree on a single figure, there is loose consensus that about four hours alone is a comfortable range for an adult dog. Puppies should only be left for shorter periods, and not longer than they can hold their bladder. Many people wonder whether dogs know the difference between being left alone for ten minutes and four hours, since dogs don't exactly watch the hands of the clock turn.

Anecdotally, people report that their dogs seem more excited and offer a more enthusiastic greeting after a longer absence. Backing this up is a study conducted by Therese Rehn and Linda Keeling, in which they observed a small group of privately owned dogs and videotaped what the dogs did before, during, and after a thirty-minute, two-hour, and four-hour separation. They found that dogs tended to offer more intense greeting behaviors, with a higher frequency of physical activity and attention behavior, after the longer separations. As they note, their study doesn't confirm whether dogs distinguish between thirty minutes and four hours, but it confirms that dogs are affected by the duration of their time alone.[17]

The surest cure for loneliness and social isolation is, of course, togetherness. To increase this, look for ways to include your dog in your activities — such as bringing your dog along when running errands or attending a child's soccer game — and build the structure of each day so that periods of isolation are broken up by together time. People sometimes complain that their lives are ruled by their dog — it's harder to go on trips, make social plans, or even get necessary work done because they have to be home to "let the dog out." Exactly. That's the reality of living with a dog, and that's why dog ownership is not right for everybody.

We also must think about the signals we send our dog. A dog trainer friend of Jessica's told her about a family who had hired him to help with a behaviorally challenged dog. The dog would cry and scratch in his downstairs kennel all night, while the family was upstairs trying to sleep through the disturbance. The trainer observed that the family and the dog spent the evenings before bed together in the living room and kitchen, playing games and watching TV. The dog was very much part of the activity and given a lot of attention. As the family got ready for bed, they gave the dog extra love and petting, and then they escorted him to the kennel, where he would spend the night separate from everyone else. The dog was being given very mixed signals; he was part of the family pack until, suddenly, he wasn't. In this case, the trainer recommended letting the dog sleep upstairs with the family. They did, and the dog was much happier, and everyone was finally able to get a good night's sleep.

Sometimes people try to address the problem of a lonely dog by bringing home a second dog so that the dogs have company even when their human is gone. This can be helpful for many dogs, and in the best cases, two or more dogs living in the same home will become best friends and add much enjoyment and enrichment to one another's lives. But adding a second dog is not a surefire cure for loneliness. The social bond between dog and human is unique; the human fills a role that cannot be filled by another dog. Studies suggest, for example, that separation anxiety is generally no better in dogs left with another dog than in those left alone. Other research shows that human social contact provides more comfort to a socially isolated dog than one of the dog's own siblings.[18] So, if you are gone for long hours each day, adding a second dog to your home may simply result in having two lonely dogs rather than one. Furthermore, multiple-dog households have their own challenges. A new dog will change the social dynamics of the family, often in ways that make things more difficult rather than easier. Dog-dog aggression can be a serious problem and can sometimes lead to untenable situations, where one dog will wind up needing to be rehomed.

DOGS ALSO NEED ALONE TIME

If you have a dog with separation anxiety, this enhancement might make you chuckle (or perhaps cry). But just like people, dogs may want to have some time to themselves. This is particularly the case in homes with children or with a lot of activity and stimulation. It is important for every dog to have a "safe zone" — a place the dog can retreat to and be allowed *not* to interact or be touched. Mishka, a somewhat zaftig husky with whom Marc shared his home, loved to nestle in a corner behind a bed when she'd had enough of her humans. She made it clear what she was doing, and there was only room for her. When she was ready to interact, she'd have to back out of her husky cave, which she did with impressive agility. Some people provide their dog with a crate or kennel — with the door always open — which is designated "dog property" and off-limits to children and other humans in the house.

Sight

We tend to think of humans as visual mammals and dogs as olfactory and auditory mammals, but science is challenging these stereotypes. The visual world we make available to our dogs is worth considering because it can impact their well-being. Let's consider the canine visual cosmos.

Visual acuity in humans is often described using what's called the Snellen fraction, which is the well-known ratio of "20/20" or "20/40" that represents the quality of one's eyesight. Dogs have a Snellen fraction of 20/75. This means that what we can see at 75 feet, a dog can see only at 20 feet. Using this method of measuring acuity, dogs have worse vision than humans. But it would be wrong to claim that dogs don't see as well as humans, since the Snellen fraction provides only one small window into the larger sense of sight. It would be more accurate to say that dogs and humans see the world differently. The visual acuity of dogs evolved to meet dogs' unique needs, and different doesn't necessarily mean better or worse.

Dogs are visual generalists, meaning that their eyes work well in a range of different light levels. They likely can see better at dusk and in the dark than humans. It's been estimated that dogs can see in light about five times dimmer than humans can. Dogs are also better adapted than humans for identifying movement in their peripheral vision. However, dogs are not as good as humans at seeing things in detail. One reason for this may be that dogs can't easily distinguish between the colors red and green.[1] A red ball thrown in a field of green grass will be challenging to see even for a Labrador retriever. Other aspects of vision include depth perception, visual field of view, and sensitivity to motion. In each of these areas, dog vision is different from human vision as visual capacities have adapted to each species' needs.

One of our mantras throughout this book is that there is no universal "dog." Dogs come in a huge variety of shapes and sizes, and their sensory capacities may vary based on these differences. In the realm of sight, for instance, different breeds appear to have different visual strengths. Alexandra Horowitz suggests that variations in canine visual acuity may be related to the shape and size of the nose. Short-nosed dogs like pugs tend to have better up-close vision, while dogs with long noses have better panoramic and peripheral vision.[2] This may help explain why short-nosed dogs are often less interested in chasing balls and Frisbees than their longer-nosed kin. It is more difficult for them to see a ball and track its movement, which makes it a lot less interesting to chase.

Many human companions report that their dog will bark at someone wearing a hat or sunglasses or walking on crutches. Dogs often get spooked by things they don't visually recognize. Loss of visual acuity is common in older dogs, just as it is in people, and dogs who are visually impaired need a little extra help interacting with their world. Their behavior may change, too. At fifteen years of age, Jessica's dog Maya has lost the use of one eye and has relatively poor vision in the other. She's started to bark at people on walks, particularly people who stand about three feet away, right in what seems to be a blind spot. Loss of vision can lead to anxiety and social withdrawal, if we aren't careful to help our canine companions adapt. That said, loss of sight, even complete blindness, does not mean that a dog has poor quality of life. Blind and visually impaired dogs can adapt quite well to their disability, though they need special care and consideration. Often these dogs adapt by relying more heavily on other sensory input, such as sound and smell, and they can be trained to follow olfactory cues or "smell hints," such as a puff of citrus essential oil.

A challenge for future research with dogs is to learn not only how each sense works on its own but how dogs combine and use the input from multiple senses — how they use composite signals — to understand the world and to make decisions. For instance, one study by dog researcher Ludwig Huber showed that captive dogs could integrate information from sight and sound to identify other dog breeds correctly. In this study, dogs matched a projected visual image of dogs of different sizes with the vocalization that is usually made by dogs of each size.[3] This kind of composite signal may help Maya determine, from quite far off, that she sees a poodle, so that she can get her hackles raised in anticipation. For whatever reason (and no offense intended), Maya is not too keen on poodles.

LET DOG-DOG INTERACTIONS FLOW

If you watch a group of dogs playing at a dog park, you will quickly notice how carefully they watch one another. Dogs will look over their shoulders as they run, or they will stop and turn around so they can see what the other dogs are doing. When they do this, they're reading body postures, gaits, tail and ear positions, facial expressions, and even watching for subtle changes in the position of another dog's fur, such as whether another dog is showing their hackles. "Hackles" refer to the hairs along a dog's neck and backbone, and "raised hackles" are called piloerection, an involuntary neural response to arousal mediated by the sympathetic nervous system. Dogs may also gather information by looking in a dog's eyes, though research in this area is limited. It may be that dilated or constricted pupils communicate something about a dog's emotional state that other dogs can decipher. In addition to this kaleidoscope of visual signals, dogs are also absorbing olfactory and auditory information, all while on the run, which is quite a remarkable feat.

It's important for dogs to be able to read one another accurately in order for social interactions to go well. The same is true in the human realm, which is one reason that highly successful people tend to be those with high levels of emotional intelligence and well-honed social skills. One of the reasons dogs can get into sticky situations with one another is when they misread visual or other signals, and some dogs are much better at reading signals than others. Spend any time at a dog park, and you will certainly notice a few dogs who are socially awkward and don't seem very good at interacting with other dogs. Oftentimes, these dogs have trouble finding play partners. Marc has noted that there often seems to be a relationship between the social skills of a dog, or lack thereof, and those of their human, but that's another story.[4]

One of the mysteries of a dog's world is how they recognize other dogs as belonging to the category "dog." Obviously, dogs recognize other dogs by smell, but they also seem able to recognize other dogs using only sight. A very interesting study conducted by Dominique Autier-Dérian and her colleagues found that dogs can identify other dogs using facial features alone, in the absence of other cues such as movement, scent, and sound. Dogs were very good at picking out the faces of other dogs, among human and other domestic and wild animal faces. C. Claiborne Ray, discussing this study, remarked, "Ranging in size from a tiny Maltese to a giant St. Bernard, and showing myriad differences in coats, snouts, ears, tails and bone structure, dogs might not always appear to belong to one species. Yet other dogs recognize them easily."[5]

We often hear dog owners say something like, "My vizsla loves other vizslas more than any other kind of dog, and she also knows they are vizslas." Can dogs really recognize other dogs of the same breed? Nobody knows, but a lot of anecdotal evidence suggests that they might. If they do, it is likely that the cues lie in the dog's olfactory sense, and perhaps in the identification of what's called the major histocompatibility complex, or MHC. The MHC is a set of surface proteins found on the cells of all mammals, and it is involved in immune function. It's thought to play a role in the selection of mates who are not too closely related genetically. The MHC may present as a kind of olfactory "signature" allowing dogs to determine genetic familiarity, but there hasn't been any research in this area. Nonetheless, many people believe their dog shows a preference for others of their same breed.

Dogs need to be able to interact with other dogs. This is what dogs are "made" for, if you will. Many of their cognitive skills and the components of their behavioral repertoire have evolved to help them communicate more effectively with others of their own kind. It is sad to think that these amazing capacities could go unused, which is why giving our dogs ample opportunity to interact with other dogs and to practice their communication skills is one of the most important forms of social and cognitive enrichment we can and must provide.

TALES ABOUT TAILS

You may wonder why tails are included in a section on sight. Well, among other things, a dog's tail is an important visual tool for communication. We can gather a lot of information about what a dog is feeling by observing their tail, and of course, tails are critical to dog-dog interactions. Looking at a tail in isolation, however, never tells the whole story; that would be like reading only part of a sentence. To fully understand what a tail is communicating, it needs to be seen in the context of a broader range of composite signals, including ear positions, facial expressions, body postures, vocalizations, odors, and gait. Tails may also be used to disperse odors, such as the scent from a dog's lovely information-packed anal gland.

Some interesting research has been done into what different tail movements are trying to communicate. As you likely know, a wagging tail can mean different things, depending on the kind of wag and the context. A loose wag is probably friendly, whereas a stiff wag likely signals assertiveness or aggression. However, there are no hard-and-fast rules.

Research has also shown that tail wagging with a bias to the right indicates that a dog is happy and relaxed, whereas left-bias wagging may indicate anxiety. In one study, dogs seeing their owners were more likely to show high-amplitude wagging with a bias to the right side (showing left-brain activation), while dogs seeing dominant unfamiliar dogs tended to wag to the left (showing right-brain activation).[6] These findings are consistent with the hypothesis that dogs have a left-hemisphere specialization for approach behavior and a right-hemisphere specialization for withdrawal behavior.

More recent research by the same group of scientists found that dogs respond emotionally to the tail-wagging bias of other dogs. The scientists analyzed the behavior and cardiac activity (a rough measure of calmness or anxiety) of a group of dogs watching images of other dogs wagging. Dogs consistently showed more pronounced emotional reactions to and were stressed by left-wagging tails.[7]

What if a dog loses their tail? Stanley Coren tells a story about a dog whose tail had to be amputated after an unfortunate dog-motorcycle collision. Other dogs seemed unable to understand what she was trying to communicate.[8] Marc's friend, Marisa Ware, told him the story of her dog, Echo, who lost her tail in an accident. After the loss, Echo changed the way she communicated with dogs and people by using her body and ears to compensate for the loss of her tail. Tailless Echo now relies more heavily on her ears to express her feelings. When she is excited to see someone, she puts her ears very far back and will almost wiggle them. She also has developed a kind of "hop-wiggle," taking a little hop and wiggling her butt very quickly if she is excited to see someone. Echo never did the "hop-wiggle" before losing her tail.

Even the shortening of a tail, such as through docking, seems to inhibit a dog's ability to communicate with other dogs. To investigate the role of tail length in dog-dog encounters, a team of researchers built remote-controlled replicas of dogs with different lengths of tail, and they observed more behavioral nuance in the reactions of dogs to long-tailed versus short-tailed replicas. This suggests that more communicative information was gleaned from a long tail, which may mean that a longer tail is more effective at sending messages than a shorter tail.[9]

The long and short of it is that tails are important to dogs. Thus, tail docking is a freedom inhibitor (and a form of disfigurement) that limits a dog's ability to communicate. We are in support of enlightened breed standards that don't involve cutting off puppies' tails.

DOGS "SPEAK" WITH THEIR EARS

Like a tail, a dog's ears are an important *visual* signal in dog-dog and dog-human interactions. The next chapter discusses hearing, while this section considers what ears say by their movement and position. Take the time to watch your dog's ears closely, since they can be a good indicator of how your dog is feeling. Ears are part of the group of composite signals — which include a dog's face, body, tail, vocalizations, gait, and odors (some of which we are only partially privy to) — that complete the sentence of what a dog is feeling.

For example, if a dog twitches their ears, moving them back and then forward a bit, it may indicate indecision or ambivalence. Pricked ears signal that a dog is paying attention. If Maya pricks her ears, Bella will immediately respond by barking. Bella's motto is "bark first, then ask why." By watching the direction another dog is turning an ear, dogs can find out information about where to look. Ear position is important during dog social encounters, including play. For example, flattened ears can signal submission if combined with submissive body posture, and "up" ears can signal excitement and intention to continue play. Flattened ears might also be a way for a dog to avoid getting them nipped.

We have been asked whether dogs like basset hounds with long, floppy ears have a harder time communicating through ear positions. It's possible that floppy ears don't allow for quite as much expressiveness, but we really don't know.[10]

As with tails, we support breed standards that don't involve cropping or otherwise changing the natural shape of a dog's ears. Doberman pinschers, Boston terriers, and Great Danes are a few of the breeds in which ear cropping is still common. During the ear-cropping procedure, the pinnae (earflaps) are altered. The pinna functions to funnel sound into the ear canal, and so dogs with cropped ears lose some acuity in their hearing; they also lose the ability to rotate the ear fully, and this makes it harder for them to communicate with their ears.

FACE THE FACTS: EXPRESSIONS MATTER

One of the composite signals dogs use to communicate includes facial expressions, and research has shown that dogs

pay particularly close attention to human facial expressions
— perhaps because we don't have tails and our ears don't
move. In one study of dogs and human facial expressions,
a team of scientists led by Corsin Müller demonstrated that
dogs differentiate between happy and angry human faces and
that dogs find angry faces to be aversive.[11] In a related study,
Natalia Albuquerque and colleagues examined the behavior
of dogs in response to emotionally relevant visual cues from
humans. The team compared the responses of dogs to happy
and angry human facial expressions and found that dogs
engaged in mouth-licking in response to angry expressions.
Dogs mouth-licked when they saw images of angry human
faces, but not when they heard angry voices, emphasizing
the importance of the visual cues. Mouth-licking can be an
appeasement signal during dog-dog communications, and it
may similarly serve as a way for a dog to respond to perceived
negative emotion in a human companion. (An "appeasement
behavior" inhibits or reduces aggressive behavior of a social
partner.) In the study, dogs engaged in mouth-licking more
often when looking at images of humans than of other dogs,
suggesting that dogs may have evolved their sensitivity to
human facial expression to facilitate interactions with us.[12]

In another study, researchers found that the hormone
oxytocin (which is associated with feelings of trust and affection) made dogs interested in smiling human faces and less
threatened by an angry face. The researchers gave half of a
group of dogs a nasal spray containing oxytocin and half a
placebo nasal spray. Those dogs with increased levels of oxytocin spent more time gazing at images of happy human faces
than dogs in the placebo group. The researchers also found

that in the placebo group, the pupils of the dogs were more dilated when gazing at angry faces, a sign that they found the angry faces aversive. In the oxytocin group this negative emotional response was less pronounced. They concluded, "Oxytocin has the potential to decrease vigilance toward threatening social stimuli and increase the salience of positive social stimuli thus making eye gaze of friendly human faces more salient for dogs."[13] In other words, oxytocin likely plays a key role in the development of the human-canine bond.

Some of the most exciting research into canine cognition has involved the use of functional Magnetic Resonance Imaging (fMRI) to study how dogs' brains process social information. This research is noninvasive, and the dogs participate voluntarily. Neurobiologist Gregory Berns, working at Emory University, has been interested in facial recognition and whether, like humans and nonhuman primates, dogs have a special region in their brain dedicated to processing faces. It would make sense that dogs evolved the neural machinery to process facial information of other dogs because dogs (and wolves) are highly social mammals. But have dogs also evolved the neural machinery to process human faces, based on their history of domestication and coevolution with humans? Berns and his colleagues found that dogs do, indeed, have a dedicated region of the brain for processing human faces, which helps explain their exquisite sensitivity to human social cues.[14]

It seems that dogs not only read our facial expressions, they also, in turn, communicate with us using their own facial expressions. Scientists at Portsmouth University's Dog Cognition Centre in the United Kingdom found that dogs produced far more facial expressions when a human was watching than when a human was not. The expression most commonly used by dogs was one in which they raise their inner brow, making the eyes appear wider and sadder, a look all dog owners will immediately recognize as "puppy dog eyes."[15] Dogs know when we're watching. And they also know when we're not. Dogs are more likely to steal food when a person's eyes are closed or their back is turned.[16]

YOUR DOG IS WATCHING: NONVERBAL COMMUNICATION AND EMOTIONAL INTELLIGENCE

When we are engaged with our dogs in a training or agility session, they're watching us very closely to see what it is we are asking them to do. But even when we are not actively working with our dogs, they're still watching us closely. They may be scanning for clues about what we are going to do next, and research suggests they're also paying close attention to our emotional state and in some cases modulating their own behavior in response to how we're feeling.

When we think about training or teaching a dog to live effectively in human environments, we may think that most of our cues are verbal: "Come," "Sit," "Stay." But verbal signals are only one small crucial component of how we communicate with dogs and of how dogs understand us. It is often said that in a human conversation as much as 60 to 90 percent or more of the interaction is nonverbal, depending on the individuals and the context.[17] We exchange information through facial expression, body posture, hand gesture, and possibly odors. The same is true for dog-human communication. We may not even be aware of all the nonverbal signals we are giving! On occasion, a dog might tell us what we're "saying" — for example, that we're angry — when we don't even realize what we're doing.[18]

How dogs read human nonverbal signals is an area of intense research, and there is much that we still don't understand well. Some of the questions under investigation include how dogs use human gestures, such as pointing, and whether and why they follow the direction of our gaze.

Following another dog's gaze is something that some dogs do quite well. Dogs can learn a good deal about what another dog is thinking when they do this, and this simple act may help demonstrate that dogs have a theory of mind — that is, that they know what another dog is thinking and feeling. Research has found that dogs also can follow human gaze, but it isn't yet clear how consistently they do this. So far, all we can safely say is that some dogs follow human gaze some of the time. Some dogs seem better at following gazes than others, or perhaps they are not "better" but more highly motivated, for whatever reason. But we don't know why. And we also don't know what other factors may be at play and what might explain the variation in experimental results. Of course, different dogs are studied in different projects with a variety of researchers, and these variables might underlie differences in research results. Expecting that all dogs will do the same things in the same or similar situations is unrealistic.

The same can be said about variations in the ability of dogs to follow human pointing gestures: Dogs are clearly able to do this, but not all dogs do it all or even some of the time, and the experimental results aren't straightforward. More research will be needed to really flesh out the details of canine communicative skills.

The one thing we do know for sure is that dogs clearly possess some level of emotional intelligence: They watch us for nonverbal cues, pay attention to our eyes and our hands, and listen to our voices, and from these things they can at times understand us quite well. Emotional intelligence is the capacity to effectively recognize and understand one's own emotions and the emotions of others and to use this information to guide one's behavior. This is important as we consider how to interact with our canine companions so as to reduce frustration on both sides. Sometimes we get frustrated when our dogs don't "listen," and they likely get frustrated with us when we don't "speak" clearly or listen to them.

When it comes to dogs following a person's gaze, we need to pay close attention to the relationship between the dog and the human. In an interesting paper called "DogTube: An Examination of Dogmanship Online," researchers suggest that "reciprocal attention in the dog-human dyad" is important in gaining a dog's attention and in handling and training them.[19] Further, they write that dogs who "are perceived as difficult to train may be in the hands of people who lack the timing and awareness that characterize good dogmanship." The researchers suggest that "dogmanship is reflected in the timeliness of rewards and the ability to acquire and retain a dog's attention when handling or training them."

It's astonishing how skilled dogs are at untangling the complicated signals we send. We expect our dogs to understand us, but our communications are garbled. Most dog owners are "messy" signalers, in that they may give a verbal command without realizing that they are also giving visual signals. We tend to blame it on the dog when they don't respond in the way we want; we think they are being stupid or stubborn. More likely, we are simply not being clear. One thing we can do to help our dogs is to approach training or teaching with an understanding of how closely dogs pay attention to all our signals, and we can try to align our verbal and nonverbal cues into a consistent and clear message.

Paying closer attention to the nonverbal aspects of training could help many people and dogs work better together. Research conducted by Anna Scandurra and colleagues suggests that gestures are more salient to dogs than verbal cues. For their study, the team trained dogs to identify one of three objects by name and retrieve the object when asked by their owner. Dogs could retrieve each object by a verbal command ("ball") or by a gesture (owner clearly pointing at ball). When verbal and gestural commands agreed, the dogs moved even more quickly to perform the task. The researchers then had owners give contradictory cues, asking for one object while pointing a finger at another. When verbal and gestural cues were different, most of the dogs followed the gesture.[20]

Thus, when it comes to our communication with dogs, visual signals, facial expressions, and nonverbal cues may be equally or even more important for dogs than verbal signals.

Hearing

D ogs' ears come in many shapes and sizes — long and short, floppy and erect, and all variations in between. Dogs' ears are surprisingly mobile. More than eighteen muscles control the pinna, or earflap, alone, which allows the nuanced movements that make dogs' ears so expressive and so good at picking up sounds. Dogs move their ears to communicate how they are feeling. They also move their ears to facilitate hearing. Every dog owner will recognize the "pricked ears" of a dog who is suddenly attentive. The up and open ears allow dogs to best capture sound. The ear muscles also allow dogs to turn their ears like a periscope to follow the direction of a sound. If we watch a dog's ears for cues, we can likely gather information about our surroundings that we would have missed. Marc used to watch his dogs' ears when hiking around their mountain home, which they of course shared with all sorts of wild animals. When there were cougars, black bears, or other potential predators around, the dogs' ears perked up and their noses often tilted upward. Marc took these responses as signals that it was time for all to head home immediately to avoid a possible confrontation.

Dogs have far more sensitive hearing than humans and can detect much quieter sounds. Their sense of hearing is about four times as sensitive as ours, so what we hear at twenty feet, a dog can hear at about eighty feet.[1] They also hear a lot of things we don't because they can hear higher-frequency sounds. From available data, scientists suggest that dogs hear in frequencies as high as 67,000 cycles per second (also called hertz), while humans hear frequencies up to 64,000 cycles per second.[2] This means there are some sounds that are inaudible to us but quite available to our dogs. For example, they can hear the high-pitched chirping of mice running around inside the walls or in the woodpile. Also, some of the electronics in our homes emit constant high-frequency sounds we don't notice but which can be distressing to dogs.

Relatively little systematic research has been done on how dogs use sound and hearing in their interactions with the world and in their encounters with people and other dogs. We know that dogs make a lot of different sounds, including growls, barks, whines, whimpers, howls, and pants, but scientists don't fully understand how these different vocalizations function in interactions with others. And we also don't know which aspects of vocal communication have evolved specifically to facilitate social interactions with humans. For instance, dogs are the only canid species to bark frequently, but perhaps surprisingly, we still don't know all that much about what dogs are trying to say with their barks. Preliminary data also suggest that dogs seem to "laugh." During play, dogs will emit a kind of forced exhalation called the "play pant," which seems to be used to initiate play and to signal during play "this is still play, and not a fight."[3] It will be fascinating to see how research into canine vocal communication evolves.

Many people use verbal commands or vocal signals to communicate with their dog. As we mention in the section on sight, dogs may pay more attention to gestures than they do to spoken commands, and they may get confused when our visual and auditory signals don't align. Researchers have also found that dogs listen not only for certain words but to tone of voice, and intonation may be more important in how dogs read a signal than the actual word spoken. Using fMRI techniques, researchers at a dog cognition lab in Hungary scanned the brains of dogs as the dogs listened to recordings of their trainers' voices. The trainers used praise words (such as "well done") and neutral words (such as "however") and spoke them in a high-pitched "good dog" voice and in a neutral voice. The results of this study showed that dogs used their left hemisphere to process the words, and their right hemisphere to process the intonation, or emotional content, of the words, which is how human brains process speech. When praise words were spoken with a praising intonation, the reward center of the brain was activated, but not when praise words were spoken with neutral intonation. In other words, dogs listen to the words and the emotional content of our speech, and the emotional content has more salience.[4]

Unlike other senses — particularly smell and taste — where pet dogs often suffer from a lack of sensory stimulation, hearing can entail the opposite problem. Dogs often suffer from too much noise or from exposure to sounds that they find aversive or frightening, which constitute serious freedom inhibitors. Of course, we should try to give our dogs the freedom to hear and communicate with sounds, but we also need to think about the overall soundscape and protect dogs from noises they don't like.

BARKS AND GROWLS: THE LANGUAGE OF DOGS

Barks and growls are two of the most common dog vocalizations, and they are used to communicate with both other dogs and humans. Vocal communication in dogs is extremely complex and not very well understood. In her analysis of dog vocalizations, German ethologist Dorit Feddersen-Petersen notes that even the meaning and function of barking is controversial. Some scientists consider barking a highly sophisticated acoustic form of expression, while others think barking is "noncommunicative."[5] Dog barking is difficult to study for a whole variety of reasons, including the fact that dogs come in a huge variety of shapes and sizes. There are big differences in the length of the vocal tract and thus in the sound quality of vocalizations. Just think of the difference between the bark of a Great Dane and of a Yorkie. Are they even speaking the same language?

Feddersen-Petersen believes that barks have definite communicative significance, and dogs use them to convey information about motivation and intention. Dog barks have a mixture of what scientists call "regular" (or harmonic) and "irregular" (or noisy) acoustic components. While wolves vocalize using noisy components only, dogs use a whole range of harmonic and noisy forms in various mixtures. Different breeds of dogs seem to have evolved unique vocal repertoires, ones based on the human environments in which they have lived. Assessing the meaning of a bark — or more accurately, a string of barks, since barks are rarely singular — is challenging and requires looking at the context and whether the bark elicits a response from a social partner (either a dog or human). It may be that barking and other vocalizations have evolved particularly to facilitate dog-human social interactions.

One way to get to know your dog better is to make an ethogram focused solely on the various barks, growls, and other sounds they use in your company and in the company of other dogs. Can you distinguish between different kinds of barks — such as sharp and high-pitched; low-pitched; coming in a steady stream or in short bursts, and so on — and can you identify what may have triggered the bark? For example, was it the postal delivery person walking by, another dog barking in the distance, or impatience because you are slow getting your shoes on for the morning walk? After studying the vocal sounds of your own dog, watch other dogs in your neighborhood or at a dog park.

Barking is a key part of the natural behavioral repertoire of dogs and is likely an important means of communication. Letting our dogs be dogs means letting them talk with one another, which means letting them vocalize. Of course, barking is often treated as a problem, and "excessive" barking — which is always defined by humans — can become a very serious issue for dog owners. A barking dog can be incredibly annoying to us and perhaps to other dogs and animals. Excessive barking is a common reason for dogs being relinquished to shelters, and it can be one of the more frustrating aspects of dog ownership. While some barking is normal, too much barking can be a sign of boredom, frustration, or stress. Trainers and dog psychologists can often help identify underlying issues that might drive excessive barking. If dog barking really bothers you, it's probably best not to get a dog.

Sometimes people deal with a dog who barks too much by having the dog's voice box surgically removed. In one particularly shocking case of "problem barking," a couple in Oregon was ordered by a court to have the voice boxes of their six dogs removed because they had failed to control the dogs' barking over ten years.[6] "Debarking" — or "bark softening," as some euphemistically (and offensively) call it — involves severing the vocal cords and is, simply put, seriously harmful to dogs. The procedure permanently eliminates one of the dog's main means of communication, which qualifies as a severe freedom inhibitor. Severing the vocal cords is never the best response to barking behavior, and a dog who has been subjected to this horrific procedure can no longer really function comfortably as a dog.

In addition to barking, dogs often growl. Whereas barks are often used to communicate at a distance, growls are generally low volume and used in close communication. Different kinds of growls carry distinct meanings and have different emotional content. For example, during play, including during tug-of-war between dogs or between a dog and a human, a dog may growl quite loudly, without showing any teeth, but this is usually meant as part of play and not to signal genuine anger or aggression. Growls produced as serious warnings will likely be low-pitched and come either from the chest or mouth, with varying levels of bared

teeth. Research has shown that dogs growl "honestly" in se-
.rious encounters (the "size" of the growl accurately reflecting
the size and aggression-level of the dog), but they show more
variability in their growling when they play. Even when dogs
growl during play, it almost never leads to fighting (less than
2 percent of the time).[7] Dogs can reliably distinguish between
a prerecorded "food growl" and a "stranger growl" and respond appropriately.[8]

Whatever else growling may mean, it clearly can be used
as a serious warning or signal of potential aggression, so we
need to pay very close attention to the rest of a dog's body language when a dog growls. Humans are not always very skilled
at reading the intention of dog growls, though people with
more experience around dogs are better at distinguishing between playful and aggressive growls, and women appear to
do better than men.[9] As with all the senses, it's important to
become dog literate and learn as much as you can about your
dog's growls. Along with a "bark ethogram," consider also
making a "growl ethogram" for your dog.

WHINING AND WHIMPERING: A CALL FOR HELP

Two other common types of vocalization are whimpering and
whining. These are distinct vocal communication patterns,
although they are sometimes hard to distinguish and many
people lump them together as "crying." Whining tends to be
louder and higher-pitched, while whimpering is quieter and
lower. Whimpering usually means that a dog isn't feeling well

and is sick, nervous, or in pain. The communicative function of whining is not as clear.

A 2017 study on the relationship between dog vocalizations and separation-related anxiety is a good example of the kind of research we need to better understand and help our dogs. Excessive barking is typically considered one of the main symptoms of separation-related disorder (SRD) in family dogs, but in this study, Péter Pongrácz and his colleagues wanted to confirm whether dogs with separation anxiety vocalize their distress through barking, through whining, or by using both vocalizations. Pongrácz's team found, contrary to popular belief, that dogs with separation anxiety were more likely to whine than to bark, particularly at the departure of their human, and that "early onset and abundance of whining may serve as a reliable tool for diagnosing SRD." Whines and barks likely reflect different inner states. Another interesting finding from Pongrácz's study was that a dog's age was the most influential factor in determining onset and abundance of barks during a short separation. Younger dogs barked sooner and more than older dogs.[10]

One common myth about "crying" in dogs is that dogs always whimper when they are in pain. While it is true that dogs in pain will sometimes whimper, they don't always vocalize their distress. A lack of whimpering does not mean a dog isn't in pain, since sometimes dogs only whimper when pain has progressed to an intolerable level. At that point, just as in humans, the cause of the pain has often progressed to a point where it is more difficult to treat. With any injury or medical problem, the ideal is to notice pain early and address the cause quickly with appropriate care or medications.

There are two lessons here: 1) If your dog is whimpering, it's possible that something is seriously wrong, so please seek the advice of a veterinarian; and 2) don't rely on vocalizations alone to determine whether your dog is uncomfortable. Be sensitive to other behavioral cues, such as body posture and mobility, and investigate any suspected problems right away.

BABY TALK AND YOUR DOG

Nearly everyone has either done it or seen it done with a dog. Someone kneels down, vigorously rubs a dog's face and head, and starts cooing and babbling: "What a sweet boy! Aren't you a sweet boy? Look at those sweet little paws! Who loves their baby, huh?" Dogs often feel like furry, excitable children, and so we use "baby talk" with them, or as scientists call it, "infant-directed speech . . . characterized by higher and more variable pitch, slower tempo and clearer articulation of vowels than in speech addressed to adults."[11]

Is this a problem? Do dogs like it or care, or do they simply tolerate it because they have no choice? And why exactly do we engage in this bizarre behavior?

A study published in 2017 tried to shed some light on pet-directed speech. The researchers learned that although people are more likely to use baby talk with young puppies, they also consistently use this speech pattern with older dogs. For their part, young puppies were more drawn to baby talk than normal human speech, while older dogs seemed to ignore it.[12]

Thus, with dogs, it seems like we sometimes prefer to treat them like children, no matter how old and mature they are. Does baby talk harm dogs? Probably not in itself. Since it nearly always expresses our affection, many dogs probably enjoy it to one degree or another. Then again, older and other dogs may find it grating and confusing, much like human adults would if spoken to that way. Observe your own dog to see what their reaction is, if anything, to this type of speech.

However, animal ethicists aren't so keen on baby talk because they say it may reinforce a tendency to "infantilize" dogs and ignore their intelligence and agency as individual beings with specific, dog-related needs, such as the need to run free with other dogs. Similar to when people dress up dogs in pink tutus or tartan sweaters, baby talk may encourage people to treat dogs like toys or dolls, as unaware objects to play with, rather than as subjective, sentient individuals.

TURN DOWN THE VOLUME: PROTECT YOUR DOG'S HEARING

With the senses of smell and taste, we've discussed how sensory deprivation can be a serious freedom inhibitor. The opposite is more often true with hearing. Our world can at times be very loud and noisy, and certain sounds can be very distressing to our canine companions, so an important freedom enhancer is to respect a dog's need for quiet and to avoid auditory overload. We might like to turn AC/DC or Spinal Tap up to eleven, but it is likely that screeching, feedback-filled rock music is actually painful to a dog's ear. If you like to play loud music — or if you do anything that creates very loud, high-pitched noise, like running a vacuum cleaner or using power tools — always make sure your dog has a place to go that is protected from the sound.

Above all, pay attention to a dog's behavior for signs that an environment is too painfully noisy for them, for whatever reason. For instance, Jessica once attended a summer Gin Blossoms concert at an outdoor venue in Fort Collins, Colorado. In theory, it was an ideal venue to bring a dog, and people were spread out on blankets and folding chairs in the grass. However, perhaps because the concert was outdoors, the sound was turned up so loud that the music was actually distorted, and Jessica had to cover her ears with her hands and leave early because the sound was physically painful. She wasn't alone. About fifteen feet away from her was a couple with their dog, who was clearly agitated, with his ears pulled back, tail down, and panting. His owners seemed totally oblivious to the dog's discomfort and showed no intentions of leaving.

Just as with people, it's also likely that dogs can suffer permanent damage and hearing loss from long-term exposure to extremely loud noises. There has been no research into noise-related canine hearing loss, but plenty of research confirms the effects on human hearing, and there's no reason to think that a dog's ears are any less sensitive to damage. It's well known that hunting dogs can experience noise-induced hearing loss. Even the sound of a single gunshot or explosion, if it occurs too close to a dog, can rupture the eardrum or damage the inner ear. Further, ear infections can also cause permanent hearing loss if not treated properly.

We owe it to our dogs to pay close attention to all the sounds we expose them to and to do what we can to protect their long-term health. However, perhaps the easiest hearing-related freedom enhancer you can provide for your dog is to silence their dog tag. If dogs could talk, that might be their number-one noise complaint. The constant jingling of the tag on their collar gets in the way of listening to the world around them, particularly when they are walking, running, or playing, and this keeps them from fully using their acute sense of hearing to experience their surroundings. Tag silencers — little neoprene covers that hold the tags together — are a cheap intervention that will be greatly appreciated by your dog.

BE SENSITIVE TO NOISE PHOBIAS

Many dog guardians know that certain sounds send their canine companion into a tizzy fit. Some of the common culprits are fireworks, gun sounds, and thunder. Indeed, studies suggest that nearly half, and perhaps as many as three-fourths, of all family dogs are afraid of certain noises and will show at least one behavioral sign of fear when exposed to them.[13] These behavioral signs include trembling, shaking, panting, salivating, hiding, and peeing or pooping in the house. These fear responses are often called noise phobias, particularly when the fear is related to a specific stimulus (such as a thunderstorm) and when the behavioral response is extreme, such as scratching through a wooden door trying to escape.

People may chuckle when they pop Bubble Wrap and their dog trembles in fright, but noise phobias are no laughing matter. The trembling is a sign of acute stress, and stress, as we know, is bad for your health. When people get genuinely scared, they sometimes joke that it "just took a year off my life!" Well, there is some truth to this, and we should take these fears seriously. Our dogs deserve it.

To help reduce the chance that noise phobias will develop, we can avoid exposing puppies to frightening sounds, and we can socialize puppies to a wide variety of sounds. There's some evidence that early exposure to a frightening sound increases the risk of developing a related phobia, so as much as possible, protect puppies from sudden or loud noises. Then, some people also find that gradual desensitization to a scary sound can help prevent phobias and, in some cases, help a dog move past their fears. As part of their puppy socialization classes, the Humane Society of Boulder Valley (Colorado) includes a gradual exposure to the sound of fireworks. A very soft recording of fireworks popping is played in the background while the puppies are given a constant stream of treats and praise. Each week the volume is increased just a bit. The puppies don't even notice the fireworks because they are so interested in getting treats and playing with the other puppies.

Despite these efforts, dogs may still develop aversions to certain sounds, and we must do our best to protect our friends from them. In addition, noise sensitivity can be an indicator of pain, so when dogs show fear or anxiety with loud noises, a visit to the veterinarian may be in order.[14] In extreme cases, dogs with noise phobias may need to see a behavioral specialist. Prescription medications may help relieve anxiety in some dogs, and they could be used prophylactically in situations where people cannot control the source of a noise, such as thunderstorms and July Fourth fireworks.[15]

DOGS NEED YOU, NOT THE RADIO

Sometimes when a dog must be left alone for long periods of time, people turn on the TV or radio, hoping that this will comfort or "entertain" the dog the way it might a person. However, this may not actually be doing a dog any favors. It's unlikely that television images — even of jumping squirrels — music, or an audiobook will be inherently interesting to them. If anything, the noise of a TV or radio might interfere with a dog's ability to hear outside sounds, which might be more important. Most dogs consider it a vital part of their job to protect their family and their home, so they may prefer to spend their day listening to "natural" sounds from outside, which are likely more interesting, stimulating, and enriching.

Leaving a radio on all day won't hurt a dog (unless the volume is too loud), and indeed, some dog trainers and veterinarians report that certain kinds of music and recorded sounds can have a calming effect and may have some application in treating separation anxiety and noise phobias.[16] But all in all, TV, radio, and music aren't substitutes for human interaction. The best treatment for separation anxiety, loneliness, and boredom is to not leave a dog alone for long periods of time.

Play

A Kaleidoscope of the Senses

We've left our discussion of social play behavior until the end because play is a kaleidoscope of the senses. Play nicely draws together our discussion of how dogs use their senses in tandem to understand and interact with the world, other dogs, and humans. Play obviously involves sight and touch, as dogs watch one another closely and chase, mouth, and wrestle with one another. Play also involves hearing and vocalizing, as dogs emit play pants and play growls, and smell must certainly play a role, since odors are all-important to dogs. That only leaves taste, which is probably least important during play, but who knows? Perhaps when dogs mouth one another they are learning more than we realize.

That said, what is play? This deceptively simple question has troubled researchers for many years. We usually think we know it when we see it, but defining social play in a way that can guide research has been tricky. Some years ago, Marc and behavioral ecologist John Byers created a definition that incorporates many of the common features of play they and others have observed among various mammals. At the time they developed this definition, John had been studying wild pigs, or peccaries, in Arizona, and Marc was studying various members of the dog family, including domestic dogs, wolves, coyotes (captive and wild), jackals, and foxes. Here is the definition they came up with:

> Social play is an activity directed toward another individual in which actions from other contexts are used in modified forms and in altered sequences. Some actions also are not performed for the same amount of time during play as they are when animals are not playing.

As you may notice, this definition centers on what animals *do* when they play; in other words, it names the structure that defines play, rather than focusing on the possible functions of play.

HOW DOGS PLAY

Defining play correctly, so that we can in fact recognize it when we see it, is the first step to understanding play's many functions, or why it's important. What this definition basically means is that play is a potpourri of different actions from different contexts, and a dog's modifications of these actions and their use out of context are what help define them as play. For example, play often involves biting, but the biting is controlled so that it doesn't cause pain or injury, as it would in the context of a fight. Restraint in play is called "self-handicapping." High-ranking dogs will also often allow themselves to be "dominated" in play, and this is called "role reversing." If this is done during play, there is no fear that they are going to be beat up or that another dog will try to usurp their position. Dogs act these ways during play because they know it's safe to do so. Canine play also has some unique behavioral elements that are not frequently seen in other contexts, such as the "play bow." This action is called a *bow* because it involves a dog crouching on their forelimbs, sticking their butt in the air, and perhaps wagging their tail or barking. The play bow is recognized by other dogs as an invitation to play.

Just like the human playground, where playing children learn important lessons about fairness and socializing, animals learn to cooperate and to play fairly when they're romping around with their friends. Research has consistently shown that animals follow four basic rules of fairness during play: *Ask first, be honest, follow the rules, and admit when you're wrong.* A lot of people get nervous when dogs play roughly, but the vast majority of play bouts among dogs are fair, and play only rarely escalates into real aggression. Melissa Shyan and her colleagues discovered that fewer than 0.5 percent of play fights in dogs developed into conflict, and only half of these were clearly aggressive encounters.[1]

If someone does something wrong while playing, dogs will correct one another with a mild rebuke that says something like, "Hey, I thought we were playing. You can't do that if you want to keep playing with me." Finally, play is always voluntary. During play, dogs can quit whenever they want to, and others often seem to know when one dog has had enough for the moment.

Of course, it can take some work to become skilled at distinguishing playful encounters from fighting, or from encounters that have an aggressive or agonistic element. We hope this chapter helps. It's unfortunate when people don't realize when play is just play and so break up a play session. People frequently do this at dog parks, for example; they misinterpret growling and barking as meaning that dogs are angry, when in fact they are only playing. Data show we need to give dogs credit for knowing what they're doing when they play. So, be a careful observer, let dogs be dogs and have lots of fun with their friends, and remember that play rarely escalates into real aggression.

THE IMPORTANCE OF PLAY

Providing our canine companions with ample opportunities to play with their friends and to meet new playmates is one of the easiest and most important enrichments we can offer. People may mistakenly believe that play, because it's fun and frivolous, is "extra" or not necessary. However, the opportunity for play — and lots of it — is crucial for a dog's happiness and well-being. In addition to being fun and enjoyable, play serves many functions and helps satisfy a whole range of biological, emotional, social, and cognitive needs.[2] It provides social and physical engagement with others that's necessary for individuals to develop the social skills they need to be card-carrying members of their species.

That is, play helps develop and maintain social bonds and skills, builds motor skills, and is a great form of aerobic and anaerobic exercise. Play is cognitively challenging because, for example, it involves animals learning how hard they can bite, how to avoid running into things as they go nuts with their playmates, and how to read the complex composite signals of other dogs and people, often while on the run.[3] Play is emotionally engaging because it makes dogs feel happy. When dogs and other animals play, they're clearly enjoying what they're doing. Animals often play just for the hell of it because it feels good. Play can also be an icebreaker and have what's called an anxiolytic effect; that is, it reduces anxiety during tense situations, thereby preventing escalation to an aggressive encounter.

For all these reasons, social play is essential for sheltered dogs, since it helps them learn the requisite social skills they need for when they're adopted and sharing a home with human companions. The organization called Dogs Playing for Life (DPFL) provides a joy-filled enrichment program that allows sheltered dogs to enjoy their time together and to romp with their friends while awaiting adoption; for an inspiring example, see DPFL's video, "The Playgroup Change," which shows how these dogs love to play.[4] As DPFL makes clear, the social skills these dogs learn are good not only for them but also for the people with whom they will live.

In addition, play helps dogs and other animals "train for the unexpected," or develop behavioral flexibility. The kaleidoscopic nature, unpredictability, and randomness of the actions that arise during play are inherent to play itself. Animals lost in play truly don't know who will do what next. Based on an extensive review of available literature on play behavior in numerous species, Marc and his colleagues Marek Špinka and Ruth Newberry have suggested that this is one reason animals play: to practice improvising when faced with novel situations. For example, humping can follow biting;

chasing can follow mouthing and wrestling; growling can follow face-licking; and at any moment, dogs may jump up, run around frenetically, and then leap at one another and wrestle once again.[5] By increasing the versatility of movements and the ability to recover from sudden shocks, such as loss of balance and falling over, play can enhance the ability of dogs to cope emotionally with unexpected stressful situations. To obtain this "training for the unexpected," dogs actively seek and create unexpected situations in play, which may be another reason why they actively put themselves into disadvantageous positions and situations.

It's especially important for puppies to play. Play is part of the natural behavioral repertoire of many infant and juvenile wild and domesticated animals, including the wild relatives of domestic dogs. Indeed, play behavior among infants and juveniles has likely evolved in a wide range of species because it helps young animals develop into more successful adults. Much the same is said about human children. Play is critical for individuals to become functional members of their species, and during childhood, it provides early training in many of the skills individuals need to learn.

PLAY IS ITS OWN REWARD: ALL PLAY IS GOOD PLAY

Some dog owners get downright angry if they arrive at the dog park and their dog refuses to play with other dogs, or they worry that something is wrong with their dog. However, remember that play is voluntary, and for a number of reasons, dogs may prefer to do something else in any given moment.

Some dogs may simply be more interested in sniffing along the fence, while other dogs may not see anyone they want to play with; dogs can be extremely picky about their playmates. There's nothing wrong with this, and a picky dog will often get coaxed into playing eventually because dog play is contagious. Of course, dogs who have not been well socialized or who have experienced past trauma may be uncomfortable around other dogs and may be reluctant to play. Tragically, some dogs who never learned how to play as puppies can struggle with it as adults. However, even with these dogs, patience, time, and opportunity are usually all that are needed for many nonplaying dogs to become players and learn to do it well.

In addition, all play is good play. It doesn't always have to involve other dogs. Dogs typically love to play with their human companions, as we enjoy playing with our dogs, whether in games of tug-of-war and hide-and-seek or in informal, improvised games, tricks, and teasing — such as a dog grabbing the ball just as their human bends down to pick it up. Although there is no research into the canine sense of humor, many people will attest that their dog does, indeed, seem to find certain things amusing.[6] Some dogs also develop games and forms of playful interactions with any other species who live in the home, whether cats or birds.

Finally, dogs also like to play by themselves. Jessica's canine friend Poppy, for example, loves to toss socks and pinecones through the air so she can chase them, and Bella will sometimes use her front paws to bury her ball in the snow so that she can hunt for it again.

One kind of solitary play activity, particularly in puppies, is what are sometimes called "zoomies." Another, more scientific term for this behavior is "frenetic random activity periods," or FRAPs. Zoomies are high-energy bursts of activity in which dogs look like they are possessed by the devil, after which they often lay down exhausted as if they've run a marathon. Dog trainer Steven Lindsay, one of the few people to write formally about zoomies, describes the behavior as solitary, spontaneous, and undirected play. He notes as follows:

> The spectacle may cause first-time dog owners to suspect that their dog has momentarily lost its mind. Dogs exhibiting such behavior appear to be possessed by a torrent of spontaneous locomotor impulses. They rush about as though careening around obstacles or fleeing from a nonexistent pursuer closing in from behind. Occasionally, a dog may appear to scramble forward faster than its body can follow, creating a hunched-up appearance as it steers wildly along its frenetic path. As the playful release reaches a climax, the dog may display a wide open-mouthed smile, wedging its ears back.[7]

Why do dogs engage in zoomies? Nobody really knows, and it may be different for each dog. Puppies seem to engage in zoomies more than adult dogs, and some dogs zoom more than others. When she was ten months old, Poppy was very much into zoomies, and Poppy's human, Sage, thinks that zoomies give Poppy an adrenaline rush. When asked what triggers Poppy to do zoomies, Sage answered, "Being a jerk." When Poppy has been teasing other dogs through a fence, stealing things from other dogs, or disobeying Sage, the zoomies begin. Jessica's older dogs don't do zoomies very often, but the one reliable trigger for both dogs is a bath. As soon as they get released from being dried off, they zoom around the house for a few minutes before collapsing in exhaustion. Another trigger for Bella is running through the tall grasses in an open field behind the local high school. Suddenly, Bella will just start to race around in playful circles and be crazy. Then, just as abruptly, she will stop and go back to the regular business of walking, as if nothing had happened.

There's no reason to try to stop zoomies, but if you have a zooming dog, make sure your dog can't get hurt by running into things that may topple or by tripping over an electric cord, and so on. And make sure to protect yourself. A superexcited dog can easily take out a kneecap. Just keep watch, step back, and keep your knees bent, so your legs can absorb the shock if your dog accidentally zooms into you.

As with so many other aspects of dog behavior, detailed studies of zoomies are sorely needed, and we look forward to seeing the results of these projects. For whoever does the research, it will certainly be a lot of fun. And, who knows, they might jump right in and zoom themselves.

In summary, it's essential that people learn how to identify play behavior in their dogs and then let their dogs play to their hearts' content. As with other types of behavior, play provides a great opportunity for us to learn about our own dog and about dogs in general. So make a play ethogram and carefully observe your dog's playful interactions. Who knows what you may discover?

The State and Future of Dogs

Captivity is the state of being for our companion dogs, and as we've stressed, captivity carries significant costs. It's not easy for dogs to live as our pets. Being "good dogs" requires a continual stream of limitations to their natural dogness. Regardless of whether dogs have "chosen" to evolve with us, they have very little choice in the specific human environments in which they live their lives, and often they have very little control over what they're allowed to do. There is a crucial asymmetry in the human-dog relationship: We enjoy many freedoms and our dogs don't. Dogs have only as much freedom as we allow them.

Because of the various constraints we place on the natural behavioral repertoire of our dogs, all pet dogs are behaviorally challenged to some degree. They are struggling to adapt, even when it seems as if they aren't. It is the obligation of every dog guardian to make this struggle a little easier, to minimize the costs of captivity and reduce the daily deprivations experienced by our dogs as they try to adapt to our homes and neighborhoods. We can do this through paying careful attention to who dogs really are and what they really need.

Our basic message, and the basic freedom enhancer we've

tried to emphasize throughout this book, is to *let your dog be a dog, as much as possible, as often as possible, and with as much patience and goodwill as possible*. As you do this, pay close attention to your dog's unique personality and idiosyncrasies. Each dog is truly a distinct individual.

As the Beatles said so well, we all get by with a little help from our friends. We sometimes forget that the human-dog friendship is two-sided. We need to hold up our end of the friendship by being proactive in providing a good life for our companions. We need to find ways to adapt ourselves and our homes *to our dogs*. Enhancements and enrichments don't fix the underlying disease of captivity, but they go a long way toward making the lives of our dogs happier and more fulfilled.

TEN WAYS TO MAKE YOUR DOG HAPPIER AND MORE CONTENT

1. Let your dog be a dog.
2. Teach your dog how to thrive in human environments.
3. Have shared experiences with your dog.
4. Be grateful for how much your dog can teach you.
5. Make life an adventure for your dog.
6. Give your dog as many choices as possible.
7. Make your dog's life interesting by providing variety in feeding, walking, and making friends.
8. Give your dog endless opportunities to play.
9. Give your dog affection and attention every day.
10. Be loyal to your dog.

People often report that their dog is their most important source of emotional support. The reason? "My dog loves me for who I am," people often reply. When we love and respect dogs for who *they* are, it is a win-win for everybody. We are most fortunate to have dogs in our lives, and we must work for the day when all dogs are fortunate to have us in their lives, too.

Acknowledgments

We both thank Jason Gardner, Monique Muhlen-kamp, and the entire crew at New World Library for their faith in this project and for their unwavering support. As usual, Jeff Campbell did a fine job of copyediting. Marc thanks Jessica for continuing to work with him and is ever grateful for her wit, novel insights, sarcasm, dark chocolate, and willingness to brainstorm. Valerie Belt, Betty Moss, and Peter Fisher continue to jam up his email inbox with references from all over the world, without which many very interesting and important sources would have remained unknown. Jessica would like to thank Marc for his ongoing collaboration, which has felt a lot more like play than work. Thanks, also, to Maya and Bella, whose companionship is unparalleled.

Notes

Introduction: Canine Captives

1. Susan Townsend, in conversation with Marc Bekoff, February 3, 2018.
2. Jennifer Arnold, *Love Is All You Need* (New York: Spiegel & Grau, 2016), 4.
3. Marc Bekoff, *The Emotional Lives of Animals* (Novato, CA: New World Library, 2007). For more discussion of how shared emotions bond dogs and humans across cultures, please see Bingtao Su, Naoko Koda, and Pim Martens, "How Japanese Companion Dog and Cat Owners' Degree of Attachment Relates to the Attribution of Emotions to Their Animals," *PLOS One* 13, no. 1 (2018), https://www.ncbi.nlm.nih.gov/pmc/articles/pmc5755896.
4. Jessica Pierce, *Run, Spot, Run* (Chicago: University of Chicago Press, 2016).
5. *PDSA Animal Wellbeing PAWS Report 2017*, pages 9–10, https://www.pdsa.org.uk/media/3290/pdsa-paw-report-2017_online-3.pdf.
6. Marc Bekoff, *Canine Confidential: Why Dogs Do What They Do* (Chicago: University of Chicago Press, 2017).
7. Marc Bekoff, "Jealousy in Dogs: Brain Imaging Shows They're Similar to Us," *Animal Emotions* (blog), *Psychology Today*, May 13, 2018, https://www.psychologytoday.com/us/blog/animal-emotions/201805/jealousy-in-dogs-brain-imaging-shows-theyre-similar-us.
8. Arnold, *Love Is All You Need*, 6.
9. One myth that survives among some people is that dogs don't feel

guilt, so making them feel guilty for doing something "wrong" really doesn't work. Suffice it to say, we don't know whether dogs feel guilt, but there are good reasons to assume they do, as do other mammals. The error stems from people misreading research conducted by Barnard College dog researcher Alexandra Horowitz (see "Disambiguating the 'Guilty Look': Salient Prompt to a Familiar Dog Behavior" in the bibliography); her work explores how people are not very good at reading guilt in a dog's facial expressions or behavior, *not* that dogs don't feel guilt. On that, the jury is still out.

10. Peter Vollmer, "Do Mischievous Dogs Reveal Their 'Guilt'?" *Veterinary Medicine/Small Animal Clinician* (June 1977): 1005.

11. The "home" may be a house or may be "on the streets," where numerous dogs actually live on their own. It's been estimated that 80 percent of dogs in the world are on their own. We also make many dogs live in the habitat of a shelter.

12. "The Shock Free Coalition PPG World Services Chat Chuckle and Share with Dr. Marc Bekoff," YouTube video, 55:12, posted by Pet Professional Guild, October 2, 2017, https://www.youtube.com/watch?v=2mosbrtzd2i&feature=youtu.be.

13. For more information on and guidelines for creating an ethogram and observing dogs, see the appendix "So, You Want to Become an Ethologist?" in Bekoff, *Canine Confidential*.

14. For an example of some of the research being conducted on the personality traits of dogs, see the University of Lincoln's "Dog Personality" website (www.uoldogtemperament.co.uk/dogpersonality). Brian Hare's Dognition website (www.dognition.com) is another great place to learn about the unique cognitive skills of your dog.

15. In "ecologically relevant" self-recognition tests based on olfaction rather than sight, dogs clearly distinguish between "me" and "you." See Ed Yong, "Can Dogs Smell Their 'Reflections'?" *The Atlantic*, August 17, 2017; Alexandra Horowitz, "Smelling Themselves: Dogs Investigate Their Own Odours Longer When Modified in an 'Olfactory Mirror' test," *Behavioural Processes* 143 (2017): 17–24; Marc Bekoff, "Observations of Scent-Marking and Discriminating Self

from Others by a Domestic Dog: Tales of Displaced Yellow Snow," *Behavioural Processes* 55 (2001): 75–79, and Bekoff, *Canine Confidential*, 123–24.

16. Ray Pierotti and Brandy Fogg, *The First Domestication: How Wolves and Humans Coevolved* (New Haven: Yale University Press, 2017), 204.

17. Helen Vaterlaws-Whiteside et al., "Improving Puppy Behavior Using a New Standardized Socialization Program," *Applied Animal Behaviour Science* 197 (2017): 55–61, and Marc Bekoff, "Giving Puppies Extra Socialization Is Beneficial for Them," *Animal Emotions* (blog), *Psychology Today*, December 1, 2017, https://www.psychologytoday.com/us/blog/animal-emotions/201712/giving-puppies-extra-socialization-is-beneficial-them.

18. D. Chapagain et al., "Aging of Attentiveness in Border Collies and Other Pet Dog Breeds: The Protective Benefits of Lifelong Training," *Frontiers in Aging Neuroscience* 9, no. 100 (2017), doi: 10.3389/fnagi.2017.00100, Marc Bekoff, "Dogs of All Ages Need to Be Challenged: Use It or Lose It," *Animal Emotions* (blog), *Psychology Today*, February 1, 2018, https://www.psychologytoday.com/blog/animal-emotions/201802/dogs-all-ages-need-be-challenged-use-it-or-lose-it.

The Field Guide to Freedoms: Exercising and Enhancing the Senses

1. The University of Doglando's enrichment center is an excellent model for others who want to establish such a program (http://doglando.com/enrichment/our-enrichment-program). Its aim is to provide pet parents with a historical perspective of what dogs were bred to do and to facilitate dogs forming close working, collaborative, and mutually respectful relationships with humans. They provide a lifestyle that allows each dog to have experiences that result in rich mental, emotional, physical, and intuitive growth, while taking into account the unique characteristics of each and every dog.

2. We discuss the knowledge translation gap in detail in our book *The*

Animals' Agenda (see bibliography). The knowledge translation gap refers to our failure to use what we know on animals' behalf.

Smell

1. Alexandra Horowitz, *Being a Dog* (New York: Scribner, 2016), is all about dogs' noses.
2. For more on a dog's nose, see Frank Rosell, *Secrets of the Snout: The Dog's Incredible Nose* (Chicago: University of Chicago Press, 2018), and Horowitz, *Being a Dog*.
3. Although dogs have superior sniffing skills compared to humans, the long-standing assumption that humans have poor olfaction turns out to be more myth than fact. The nineteenth-century anatomist Paul Broca noted that humans have a small olfactory bulb, relative to overall brain size compared to other mammals, and interpreted this to mean that we relied very little on our olfactory sense — that we are "nonsmellers" and that we suffer from what later came to be called *microsmaty*, or "tiny smell" (a defect that Freud thought made humans susceptible to mental illness). Broca's dismissal of the human sense of smell led to an overall scientific neglect of this human sensory skill. New research in neuroscience suggests that the human olfactory system may be just as complex and discriminating as that of other mammals. See John P. McGann, "Poor Human Olfaction Is a 19th-Century Myth," *Science* 356 (May 12, 2017): 597, http://science.sciencemag.org/content/356/6338/eaam7263.
4. Horowitz, *Being a Dog*, 48.
5. Having a compromised sense of smell is only one of the potential issues faced by brachycephalic or short-snouted dogs. Because the upper jaw of the skull has been compressed (through selective breeding), the soft tissue of the nasal passage is crammed within the skull, and this can lead to difficulty breathing. These dogs are at high risk of developing brachycephalic obstructive airway syndrome, which can be life threatening for the dog and expensive for the owner. Several studies have shown that many owners of brachycephalic dogs do

not believe their dogs have breathing problems, despite clear physical symptoms. Instead, they think that the snorting and snuffling sounds made as the dog breathes are just "normal" for "this kind of dog."

Veterinary groups are concerned about the increasing popularity of some brachycephalic breeds. For example, Kennel Club registrations of French bulldogs shot up from 692 in 2007 to 21,470 in 2016. The British Veterinary Association has launched a campaign to educate prospective and current owners of these short-nosed breeds about how to identify common health problems. Prospective owners are encouraged to consider a different breed altogether or a crossbreed, or to look for healthier versions of the brachycephalic breeds, which have been bred to have slightly longer snouts.

See, for example, Nicola Davis, "Think Twice about Buying 'Squashed-Faced Breeds,' Vets Urge Dog-Lovers," *Guardian*, January 5, 2018, https://www.theguardian.com/lifeandstyle/2018/jan/05/think-twice-about-buying-squashed-faced-breeds-vets-urge-dog-lovers; and Royal Veterinary College, "Worrying Numbers of 'Short-Nosed' Dog Owners Do Not Believe Their Pets to Have Breathing Problems," *Phys-Org*, May 10, 2012, https://phys.org/news/2012-05-short-nosed-dog-owners-pets-problems.html.

6. Horowitz, *Being a Dog*.
7. Sophia Yin, in *Secret Science of the Dog Park*, directed by Jeremy Nelson (Canada: Stornoway Productions, 2015); see Bekoff, "Dog Park Confidential," chap. 8 in *Canine Confidential*.
8. Nancy Kerns, "Walking the Dog On Leash: Why Is It So Hard for People?" *Whole Dog Journal*, October 22, 2017, https://www.whole-dog-journal.com/blog/walking-the-dog-on-leash-dragging-pulling-21725-1.html.
9. Because dogs failed the so-called "mirror test" developed by Gordon Gallup in the 1970s to test self-recognition in chimpanzees, it was long assumed that dogs didn't have a sense of "self" as separate from "other." But in "ecologically relevant" self-recognition tests based on olfaction, dogs clearly distinguish between "me" and "you." See Introduction, note 15.
10. Marc Bekoff, "Butts and Noses: Secrets and Lessons from Dog Parks,"

Animal Emotions (blog), *Psychology Today*, May 16, 2015, https://www
.psychologytoday.com/us/blog/animal-emotions/201505/butts-and
-noses-secrets-and-lessons-dog-parks; and Marc Bekoff,
"Scent-Marking by Free Ranging Domestic Dogs: Olfactory and
Visual Components," *Biology of Behavior* 4 (1979): 123–39; also see
Bekoff, "Who's Walking Whom," chap. 5 in *Canine Confidential.*

11.   See Fear Free (https://fearfreepets.com); and Janice K. F. Lloyd,
"Minimising Stress for Patients in the Veterinary Hospital: Why It Is
Important and What Can Be Done about It," *Veterinary Sciences* 4,
no. 2 (June 2017), https://www.ncbi.nlm.nih.gov/pmc/articles
/pmc5606596.

12.   Marc Bekoff, "Dogs' Noses in the News: Scents Reduce Stress in
Shelters," *Animal Emotions* (blog), *Psychology Today*, April 21, 2018,
https://www.psychologytoday.com/us/blog/animal-emotions/201804
/dogs-noses-in-the-news-scents-reduce-stress-in-shelters.

Taste

1.   The ethics of what — or who — to feed our dogs is complicated. It
is worth noting that many dog owners are "animal lovers" who, for
themselves, have chosen a plant-based diet. Some of these people feel
uncomfortable feeding meat to their dogs because of the suffering
imposed on farm animals, but they do so anyway because they
believe that dogs need meat in their diet to be healthy. Others decide
to feed their dogs a vegan diet, whether homemade or one of the few
commercially available vegan kibbles. Dogs are omnivores and can
likely have their nutritional needs met by a vegan or vegetarian diet.
But there isn't yet much scientific research into what the ideal vegan
dog diet would look like or how it would affect a dog's long-term
health; adequate data do not yet exist that speak to the question of
whether vegetarian or vegan dogs have lower-quality lives or die
younger.

2.   M. Arendt et al., "Diet Adaptation in Dog Reflects Spread of

Prehistoric Agriculture," *Heredity* 117, no. 5 (November 2016): 301–6, https://www.ncbi.nlm.nih.gov/pmc/articles/pmc5061917.

3. This *Slate* essay describes the flehmen response and, more importantly, includes a link to a variety of images of animals making the flehmen face: Jason Bittel, "Why Do Dogs, Cats, Camels, and Llamas Make That Weird Face?" *Slate*, January 12, 2016, http://www.slate.com/blogs/wild_things/2016/01/12/dogs_cats_and_other_animals_flehmen_response_to_smell.html.

4. Ian Billinghurst, *Give Your Dog a Bone: The Practical Commonsense Way to Feed Dogs for a Long Healthy Life* (Mundaring, Western Australia: Warrigal Publishing, 1993).

5. Benjamin Hart et al., "The Paradox of Canine Conspecific Coprophagy," *Veterinary Medicine and Science* (2018), doi: 10.1002/vms3.92.

6. Emily Underwood, "Scientists Discover a Sixth Sense on the Tongue — for Water," *Science*, May 30, 2017, http://www.sciencemag.org/news/2017/05/scientists-discover-sixth-sense-tongue-water.

7. Stanley Coren, "How Good Is Your Dog's Sense of Taste?" *Canine Corner* (blog), *Psychology Today*, April 19, 2011, https://www.psychologytoday.com/blog/canine-corner/201104/how-good-is-your-dogs-sense-taste.

8. For example, see Carl Engelking, "How Dogs Drink Revealed in Super Slo-Mo Video," *Discover*, November 25, 2014, http://blogs.discovermagazine.com/d-brief/2014/11/25/how-dogs-drink-revealed-in-super-slo-mo-video/#.wl1e5n-nguk.

9. Many people, when they think of dogs salivating at the smell of food, call to mind the work of Russian physiologist Ivan Pavlov and his research on dogs. Pavlov distinguished between "unconditional" salivating that occurred when food was presented and salivating as a "conditional reflex" in response to a lab technician in a white coat — something that had become associated with food — even when no food was present. Unfortunately for Pavlov's dogs, his research methods were barbaric. For the record, he never trained a dog to salivate to the sound of a ringing bell — something for which Pavlov is famous. For a quick review, see Michael Specter, "Drool: Ivan

Pavlov's Real Quest," *New Yorker*, November 24, 2014, https://www
.newyorker.com/magazine/2014/11/24/drool.

10.   Barbara King, "Dogs and Pigs Get Bored, Too," *National Public Radio*,
August 10, 2017, https://www.npr.org/sections/13.7/2017/08/10
/542438808/dogs-and-pigs-get-bored-too.

11.   Michael W. Fox, *Laboratory Animal Husbandry: Ethology, Welfare,
and Experimental Variables* (Albany: State University of New York
Press, 1986), 117–18.

12.   For UK statistics, see Alexander J. German et al., "Dangerous Trends
in Pet Obesity," *Veterinary Record* 182 (2018), https://veterinaryrecord
.bmj.com/content/182/1/25.1. For US statistics, see the Association for
Pet Obesity Prevention website, https://petobesityprevention.org.

13.   Eleanor Parker, "How Your Dog's Food Affects His Mood," Australian
Dog Lover, April 2018, http://www.australiandoglover.com/2018/04
/how-your-dogs-food-affects-his-mood.html.

14.   Jessica Pierce, "Is Your Dog a Stress-Eater?" *All Dogs Go to Heaven*
(blog), *Psychology Today*, March 27, 2018, https://www.psychology
today.com/us/blog/all-dogs-go-heaven/201803/is-your-dog-stress
-eater.

15.   Eleanor Raffan et al., "A Deletion in the Canine POMC Gene Is
Associated with Weight and Appetite in Obesity-Prone Labrador Retriever Dogs," *Cell Metabolism* 23 (2016): 893–900. See also Alexander
Bates, "Why Are so Many Labradors Fat?" *New Scientist*, May 4, 2016,
https://www.newscientist.com/article/2086840-why-are-so-many
-labradors-fat.

16.   Carly Hodes, "More Fat, Less Protein Improves Detection Dogs'
Sniffers," *Cornell Chronicle*, March 21, 2013, http://news.cornell.edu
/stories/2013/03/more-fat-less-protein-improves-detection-dogs
-sniffers.

Touch

1.   San Francisco SPCA, "Prong Collar Myths and Facts," accessed September 7, 2018, https://www.sfspca.org/prong/myths.

2. Zazie Todd, "What Is Positive Punishment in Dog Training?" *Companion Animal Psychology* (blog), October 25, 2017, https://www .companionanimalpsychology.com/2017/10/what-is-positive -punishment-in-dog.html.

3. Laura Goldman, "Cruel Shock Collars Are Now Banned in Scotland, But Still Not in the US," Care2.com, February 27, 2018, https://www .care2.com/causes/cruel-shock-collars-now-banned-in-scotland-but -still-not-in-the-us.html.

4. David Grimm, "These May Be the World's First Images of Dogs — and They're Wearing Leashes," *Science*, November 16, 2017, http://www.sciencemag.org/news/2017/11/these-may-be-world-s -first-images-dogs-and-they-re-wearing-leashes.

5. Jessica Pierce, "Not Just Walking the Dog," *All Dogs Go to Heaven* (blog), *Psychology Today*, March 16, 2017, https://www.psychology today.com/blog/all-dogs-go-heaven/201703/not-just-walking -the-dog.

6. *PDSA Animal Wellbeing PAWS Report 2017*, page 11, https://www .pdsa.org.uk/media/3290/pdsa-paw-report-2017_online-3.pdf.

7. Thomas Fletcher and Louise Platt, "(Just) a Walk with the Dog? Animal Geographies and Negotiating Walking Spaces," *Social and Cultural Geography* (2018), https://www.tandfonline.com/doi/full/10 .1080/14649365.2016.1274047.

8. See "Dog Parks Lead Growth in U.S. City Parks," Trust for Public Land, April 15, 2015, https://www.tpl.org/media-room/dog-parks -lead-growth-us-city-parks; and "2014 City Park Facts," 2014, Trust for Public Land, https://www.tpl.org/2014-city-park-facts. This website contains numerous details about many different aspects of urban parks.

9. Information on the history of dog parks can be found in Laurel Allen, "Dog Parks: Benefits and Liabilities," Master's capstone project, University of Pennsylvania, May 29, 2007, http://repository.upenn .edu/cgi/viewcontent.cgi?article=1017&context=mes_capstones; and Haya El Nasser, "Fastest-Growing Urban Parks Are for the Dogs," *USA Today*, December 8, 2011, http://usatoday30.usatoday.com/news /nation/story/2011-12-07/dog-parks/51715340/1.

10.   See Samantha Bartram, "All Dogs Allowed," *Parks and Recreation*, National Recreation and Park Association, January 1, 2014, https://www.nrpa.org/parks-recreation-magazine/2014/january /all-dogs-allowed; and F. Gaunet, E. Pari-Perrin, and G. Bernardin, "Description of Dogs and Owners in Outdoor Built-Up Areas and Their More-Than-Human Issues," *Environmental Management* 54, no. 3 (2014): 383–401, doi: 10.1007/s00267-014-0297-8.

11.   Zsuzsa Ákos et al., "Leadership and Path Characteristics during Walks Are Linked to Dominance Order and Individual Traits in Dogs," *PLOS Computational Biology* 10, no. 1 (2014): e1003446, https://doi.org/10.1371/journal.pcbi.1003446.

12.   Patricia McConnell, "A New Look at Play Bows," *The Other End of the Leash* (blog), March 28, 2016, http://www.patriciamcconnell.com /theotherendoftheleash/a-new-look-at-play-bows.

13.   See Edward T. Hall, *The Hidden Dimension* (New York: Anchor Books, 1986), which is a classic work on personal space and proxemics.

14.   See "Pekingese," CyberPet, accessed September 8, 2018, http://www .cyberpet.com/dogs/pekingese.htm.

15.   Ceylan Yeginsu, "U.K. Appoints a Minister for Loneliness" *New York Times*, January 17, 2018, https://www.nytimes.com/2018/01/17/world /europe/uk-britain-loneliness.html.

16.   "Number of Hours Pet Dogs Left Alone in the House in the United Kingdom (UK) in 2013," Statista, https://www.statista.com/statistics /299859/dogs-hours-left-alone-in-the-united-kingdom-uk.

17.   Therese Rehn and Linda J. Keeling, "The Effect of Time Left Alone at Home on Dog Welfare," *Applied Animal Behaviour Science* 129 (2011): 129–35.

18.   David S. Tuber et al., "Behavioral and Glucocorticoid Responses of Adult Domestic Dogs (*Canis familiaris*) to Companionship and Social Separation," *Journal of Comparative Psychology* 110 (1996): 103–8, https://www.researchgate.net/profile/michael_hennessy5 /publication/14352984_behavioral_and_glucocorticoid_responses _of_adult_domestic_dogs_canis_familiaris_to_companionship _and_social_separation.

Sight

1. Marcello Siniscalchi et al., "Are Dogs Red–Green Colour Blind?" *Royal Society Open Science* 4 (November 2017), doi: 10.1098/rsos .170869.

2. Horowitz, *Being a Dog*, 204–5.

3. Ludwig Huber, "How Dogs Perceive and Understand Us," *Current Directions in Psychological Science* 25, no. 5 (2016), http://journals .sagepub.com/doi/abs/10.1177/0963721416656329.

4. Bekoff, *Canine Confidential*. Marc has also noted a relationship between the personality of humans and how permissive they are in allowing their dog to interact with unfamiliar dogs. Namely, outgoing people seem more permissive than introverted people. Of course, these are only informal observations that require more formal study. However, when he has talked with other people at dog parks, they have agreed with this trend.

5. Dominique Autier-Dérian et al., "Visual Discrimination of Species in Dogs (*Canis familiaris*)" *Animal Cognition* 16, no. 4 (July 2013), https://www.ncbi.nlm.nih.gov/pubmed/23404258.

6. A. Quaranta, M. Siniscalchi, and G. Vallortigara, "Asymmetric Tail-Wagging Responses by Dogs to Different Emotive Stimuli," *Current Biology* 17 (2007): R199–R201.

7. Marcello Siniscalchi, Rita Lusito, Giorgio Vallortigara, and Angelo Quaranta, "Seeing Left- or Right-Asymmetric Tail Wagging Produces Different Emotional Responses in Dogs," *Current Biology* 23 (2013): 2279–82.

8. Stanley Coren, "Long Tails Versus Short Tails and Canine Communication," *Canine Corner* (blog), *Psychology Today*, February 1, 2012, https://www.psychologytoday.com/blog/canine-corner/201202/long -tails-versus-short-tails-and-canine-communication.

9. See S. D. A. Leaver and T. E. Reimchen, "Behavioural Responses of *Canis familiaris* to Different Tail Lengths of a Remotely-Controlled Life-Size Dog Replica," *Behaviour* 145 (2007): 377–90, http://web.uvic .ca/~reimlab/robodog.pdf.

10. People often wonder why some dogs have floppy ears in the first

place, since none of their wild canid relatives do. Here is one interesting hypothesis for why floppy ears may have developed in dogs and other domesticated animals: Adam Cole, "Why Dogs Have Floppy Ears: An Animated Tale," *NPR*, January 30, 2018, https://www.npr.org/2018/01/30/580806947/why-dogs-have-floppy-ears-an-animated-tale. The NPR story is based on this study: Adam S. Wilkins, Richard W. Wrangham, and W. Tecumseh Fitch, "The 'Domestication Syndrome' in Mammals: A Unified Explanation Based on Neural Crest Cell Behavior and Genetics," *Genetics* 197 (2014): 795–808, http://www.genetics.org/content/197/3/795.

11. Corsin A. Müller et al., "Dogs Can Discriminate Emotional Expressions of Human Faces," *Current Biology* 25, no. 5 (February 2015), http://www.cell.com/current-biology/abstract/s0960-9822(14)01693-5.

12. Natalia Albuquerque et al., "Mouth-Licking by Dogs as a Response to Emotional Stimuli," *Behavioural Processes* 146 (January 2018), https://www.ncbi.nlm.nih.gov/pubmed/29129727. See also Angelika Firnkes et al., "Appeasement Signals Used by Dogs During Dog-Human Communication," *Journal of Veterinary Behavior* 19 (2017): 35–44.

13. Sanni Somppi et al., "Nasal Oxytocin Treatment Biases Dogs' Visual Attention and Emotional Response toward Positive Human Facial Expressions," *Frontiers in Psychology* 8 (2017), https://www.ncbi.nlm.nih.gov/pubmed/29089919.

14. Daniel D. Dilks et al., "Awake fMRI Reveals a Specialized Region in Dog Temporal Cortex for Face Processing," *PeerJ* (August 4, 2015), https://peerj.com/articles/1115.

15. Juliane Kaminski et al., "Human Attention Affects Facial Expressions in Domestic Dogs," *Scientific Reports* 7 (October 2017): 12914, https://www.ncbi.nlm.nih.gov/pubmed/29051517.

16. J. Call et al., "Domestic Dogs (*Canis familiaris*) Are Sensitive to the Attentional State of Humans," *Journal of Comparative Psychology* 117 (2003): 257–63.

17. Blake Eastman, "How Much of Communication Is Really Nonverbal?" The Nonverbal Group, accessed September 8, 2018, http://www.nonverbalgroup.com/2011/08/how-much-of-communication-is

-really-nonverbal. Our point here simply is to note that a good deal of information can be transmitted without words.

18.   Marc Bekoff, "Can Dogs Tell Us We're Angry When We Don't Know We Are?" *Animal Emotions* (blog), *Psychology Today*, November 30, 2017, https://www.psychologytoday.com/blog/animal-emotions /201711/can-dogs-tell-us-were-angry-when-we-dont-know-we-are.

19.   Elyssa Payne, Pauleen Bennett, and Paul McGreevy, "DogTube: An Examination of Dogmanship Online," *Journal of Veterinary Behavior* 17 (2017): 50–61, http://www.journalvetbehavior.com/article/s1558 -7878(16)30167-8/abstract.

20.   Anna Scandurra et al., "Should I Fetch One or the Other?: A Study on Dogs on the Object Choice in the Bimodal Contrasting Paradigm," *Animal Cognition* 21, no. 1 (November 2017), https://link .springer.com/article/10.1007%2fs10071-017-1145-z.

Hearing

1.   Beth McCormick, "Fido Can Hear You, but Is He Really Listening?" Starkey Hearing Technologies, November 1, 2017, https://www .starkey.com/blog/2017/11/can-my-dog-understand-me.

2.   George M. Strain, "How Well Do Dogs and Other Animals Hear?" Deafness in Dogs & Cats (Louisiana State University), last updated April 10, 2017, https://www.lsu.edu/deafness/hearingrange.html.

3.   P. R. Simonet, M. Murphy, and A. Lance, "Laughing Dog: Vocalizations of Domestic Dogs during Play Encounters," paper presented at the meeting of the Animal Behavior Society, Corvallis, OR, 2001.

4.   A. Andics et al., "Neural Mechanisms for Lexical Processing in Dogs," *Science* 353 (September 2016): 1030–32, http://science.sciencemag.org /content/353/6303/1030.

5.   Dorit Feddersen-Petersen, "Communication — Vocal: Communication in Dogs and Wolves," in *Encyclopedia of Animal Behavior*, ed. Marc Bekoff (Westport, CT: Greenwood Press, 2004), 385–94.

6.   Aimee Green, "Owners Must Surgically 'Debark' Loud Dogs, Court Rules," *Oregonian*, August 31, 2017, http://www.oregonlive.com

/pacific-northwest-news/index.ssf/2017/08/owners_must_surgically
_debark.html.

7. Bekoff, "A Dog Companion's Guide," chap. 9 in *Canine Confidential.*

8. Tamás Faragó, "Dog (*Canis familiaris*) Growls as Communicative
    Signals" (PhD thesis, Eötvös Loránd University, Budapest, 2011),
    http://teo.elte.hu/minosites/ertekezes2011/farago_t.pdf.

9. Tamás Faragó et al., "Dog Growls Express Various Contextual and
    Affective Content for Human Listeners," *Royal Society Open Science* 4
    (May 17, 2017): 170134, doi: 10.1098/rsos.170134.

10. Péter Pongrácz et al., "Should I Whine or Should I Bark?: Qualitative
    and Quantitative Differences between the Vocalizations of Dogs
    with and without Separation-Related Symptoms," *Applied Animal
    Behaviour Science* 196 (November 2017): 61–68, doi: 10.1016/j
    .applanim.2017.07.002.

11. Tobey Ben-Aderet et al., "Dog-Directed Speech: Why Do We Use It
    and Do Dogs Pay Attention to It?" *Proceedings of the Royal Society B*
    284 (January 11, 2017), http://rspb.royalsocietypublishing.org/content
    /284/1846/20162429.

12. Ibid.

13. Emily Blackwell, John Bradshaw, and Rachel Casey, "Fear Responses
    to Noises in Domestic Dogs: Prevalence, Risk Factors, and Co-
    occurrence with Other Fear Related Behaviour," *Applied Animal
    Behaviour Science* 145 (2013): 15–25, https://www.applied
    animalbehaviour.com/article/s0168-1591(12)00367-x/abstract. See
    also Katriina Tiira, Sini Sulkama, and Hannes Lohi, "Prevalence,
    Comorbidity, and Behavioral Variation in Canine Anxiety," *Journal of
    Veterinary Behavior* 16 (2016): 36–44, https://pdfs.semanticscholar
    .org/a3de/432e01cbfbc60c17a662219d6262344b2451.pdf.

14. "Dogs with Noise Sensitivity Should Be Routinely Assessed for Pain
    by Vets," Phys-Org, March 20, 2018, https://phys.org/news/2018-03
    -dogs-noise-sensitivity-routinely-pain.html.

15. M. Korpivaara et al., "Dexmedetomidine Oromucosal Gel for
    Noise-Associated Acute Anxiety and Fear in Dogs: A Randomised,
    Double-Blind, Placebo-Controlled Clinical Study," *Veterinary Record*

180, no. 14 (April 8, 2017), https://www.ncbi.nlm.nih.gov/pubmed /28213531.

16. "Research," iCalmPet, accessed September 8, 2018, https://icalmpet .com/about/music/research.

Play: A Kaleidoscope of the Senses

1. Melissa R. Shyan, Kristina A. Fortune, and Christine King, "'Bark Parks': A Study on Interdog Aggression in a Limited-Control Environment," *Journal of Applied Animal Welfare Science* 6, no. 1 (2003): 25–32, http://freshairtraining.com/pdfs/barkparks.pdf. Although Marc and his students didn't keep detailed records on this aspect of play for dogs, they observed that play didn't turn into serious fighting more than around 2 percent of the time among the thousands of play bouts they observed. Current observations at dog parks around Boulder, Colorado, support this conclusion. Additionally, he and his students observed numerous play bouts among wild coyotes, mainly youngsters, and on only about five occasions did they see play fighting escalate into serious fighting.

2. For a detailed discussion of dogs' needs, see Linda Michaels, *Do No Harm: Dog Training and Behavior Manual* (2017), https://gumroad .com/lindamichaels; and Linda Michaels, "Hierarchy of Dog Needs," Del Mar Dog Training, http://www.dogpsychologistoncall.com /hierarchy-of-dog-needs-tm.

3. Rebecca Sommerville, Emily A. O'Connor, and Lucy Asher, "Why Do Dogs Play?: Function and Welfare Implications of Play in the Domestic Dog," *Applied Animal Behaviour Science* 197 (2017): 1–8.

4. For more information, see Marc Bekoff, "The Power and Importance of Social Play for Sheltered Dogs," *Animal Emotions* (blog), *Psychology Today*, July 28, 2018, https://www.psychologytoday.com/us/blog /animal-emotions/201807/the-power-and-importance-social-play -sheltered-dogs. See also the website Dogs Playing for Life (https://dogsplayingforlife.com) and their video "The Playgroup

Change" (https://drive.google.com/file/d/1arizcmufkqi3vjezamt9n
hc5ljtbx2fp/view).

5. Marek Špinka, Ruth Newberry, and Marc Bekoff, "Mammalian Play:
Training for the Unexpected," *Quarterly Review of Biology* 76 (2001):
141–68, https://www.ncbi.nlm.nih.gov/pubmed/11409050. See also
Marc Bekoff, "How and Why Dogs Play Revisited: Who's Confused?"
Animal Emotions (blog), *Psychology Today*, November 29, 2015,
https://www.psychologytoday.com/blog/animal-emotions/201511
/how-and-why-dogs-play-revisited-who-s-confused.

6. Bekoff, "Dogs Just Want to Have Fun," chap. 3 in *Canine Confidential*.

7. Steven Lindsay, ed., *Handbook of Applied Dog Behavior and Training*,
vol. 3 (Ames, IA: Iowa State Press, 2005), 322.

Bibliography

Here are some key references for the topics we've discussed. Many have been cited in the text, and others are included to indicate the broad range of research that has been done on dogs, their wild relatives, and other animals.

Abbott, Elizabeth. *Dogs and Underdogs: Finding Happiness at Both Ends of the Leash.* New York: Viking, 2015.

Abrantes, Roger. *Dog Language: An Encyclopedia of Canine Behaviour.* Ann Arbor, MI: Wakan Tanka, 2009.

Allen, Laurel. "Dog Parks: Benefits and Liabilities." Master's capstone project, University of Pennsylvania, May 29, 2007. http://repository .upenn.edu/cgi/viewcontent.cgi?article=1017&context=mes _capstones.

Andics, A., A. Gábor, M. Gácsi, T. Faragó, D. Szabó, and Á. Miklósi. "Neural Mechanisms for Lexical Processing in Dogs." *Science* 353 (September 2016): 1030–32. http://science.sciencemag.org/content/early /2016/08/26/science.aaf3777.

Archer, John. "Why Do People Love Their Pets?" *Evolution and Human Behavior* 18 (1997): 237–59. http://courses.washington.edu/evpsych /archer_why-do-people-love-their-pets_1997.pdf.

Arden, Rosalind, and Mark James Adams. "A General Intelligence Factor in Dogs." *Intelligence* 55 (2016): 79–85. http://www.sciencedirect.com /science/article/pii/S016028961630023x.

Arden, Rosalind, Miles K. Bensky, and Mark J. Adams. "A Review of Cognitive Abilities in Dogs, 1911 through 2016: More Individual Differences, Please!" *Current Directions in Psychological Science* 25, no. 5 (2016): 307–12. http://journals.sagepub.com/doi/full /10.1177/0963721416667718.

Arnold, Jennifer. *Love Is All You Need*. New York: Spiegel & Grau, 2016.

Artelle, K. A., L. K. Dumoulin, and T. E. Reimchen. "Behavioural Responses of Dogs to Asymmetrical Tail Wagging of a Robotic Dog Replica." *Laterality* 16 (2011): 129–35. http://www.ncbi.nlm.nih.gov/pubmed /20087813.

Arthur, Nan Kené. *Chill Out Fido!: How to Calm Your Dog*. Wenatchee, WA: Dogwise Publishing, 2009.

Autier-Dérian, Dominique, Bertrand L. Deputte, Karine Chalvet-Monfray, Marjorie Coulon, and Luc Mounier. "Visual Discrimination of Species in Dogs (*Canis familiaris*)." *Animal Cognition* 16, no. 4 (July 2013): 637–51. https://www.ncbi.nlm.nih.gov/pubmed/23404258.

Bálint, Anna, Tamás Faragó, Antal Dóka, Ádám Miklósi, and Péter Pongrácz. "'Beware, I Am Big and Non-Dangerous!'—Playfully Growling Dogs Are Perceived Larger Than Their Actual Size by Their Canine Audience." *Applied Animal Behaviour Science* 148, nos. 1–2 (2013): 128–37. https://www.sciencedirect.com/science/article/pii /S0168159113001871.

Ball, Philip. "Don't Be Sniffy If You Smell like a Dog." *Guardian*. May 14, 2017. https://www.theguardian.com/science/2017/may/14 /dont-be-sniffy-if-you-smell-like-a-dog.

Bartram, Samantha. "All Dogs Allowed." *Parks and Recreation*. National Recreation and Park Association. January 1, 2014. https://www.nrpa .org/parks-recreation-magazine/2014/january/all-dogs-allowed.

Bauer, Erika, and Barbara Smuts. "Cooperation and Competition during Dyadic Play in Domestic Dogs, *Canis familiaris*." *Animal Behaviour* 73 (2007): 489–99. http://psycnet.apa.org/psycinfo/2007-03752-013.

Beaver, Bonnie. *Canine Behavior: Insights and Answers*. 2nd ed. St. Louis: Saunders Elsevier, 2009.

Becker, Marty, Lisa Radosta, Wailani Sung, and Mikkel Becker. *From Fearful to Fear Free*. Deerfield Beach, FL: Health Communications, 2018.

Bekoff, Marc. *Animal Emotions: Do Animals Think and Feel?* (blog). *Psychology Today*, 2009–present. https://www.psychologytoday.com /blog/animal-emotions.

——. "Anthropomorphic Double-Talk: Can Animals Be Happy but Not Unhappy? No!" *Animal Emotions* (blog). *Psychology Today*, June 24, 2009. https://www.psychologytoday.com/blog/animal-emotions /200906/anthropomorphic-double-talk-can-animals-be-happy-not -unhappy-no.

——. "Bowsers on Botox: Dogs Get Eye Lifts, Tummy Tucks, and More." *Animal Emotions* (blog). *Psychology Today*, March 23, 2017. https://www.psychologytoday.com/blog/animal-emotions/201703 /bowsers-botox-dogs-get-eye-lifts-tummy-tucks-and-more.

——. *Canine Confidential: Why Dogs Do What They Do.* Chicago: University of Chicago Press, 2017.

——. "Do Dogs Ever Simply Want to Die to End the Pain?" *Animal Emotions* (blog). *Psychology Today*, December 17, 2015. https://www .psychologytoday.com/blog/animal-emotions/201512/do-dogs-ever -simply-want-die-end-the-pain.

——. "Do Dogs Really Bite Someone for 'No Reason at All'? Take Two." *Animal Emotions* (blog). *Psychology Today*, December 5, 2016. https://www.psychologytoday.com/blog/animal-emotions/201612 /do-dogs-really-bite-someone-no-reason-all-take-two.

——. "Do Dogs Really Feel Guilt or Shame? We Really Don't Know." *Animal Emotions* (blog). *Psychology Today*, March 23, 2014. https://www.psychologytoday.com/blog/animal-emotions/201403 /do-dogs-really-feel-guilt-or-shame-we-really-dont-know.

——. "Dogs and Guilt: We Simply Don't Know." *Animal Emotions* (blog). *Psychology Today*, February 9, 2018. https://www.psychology today.com/blog/animal-emotions/201802/dogs-and-guilt-we-simply -dont-know.

——. "Dogs: Do 'Calming Signals' Always Work or Are They a Myth?" *Animal Emotions* (blog). *Psychology Today*, June 25, 2017. https://www.psychologytoday.com/us/blog/animal-emotions/201706 /dogs-do-calming-signals-always-work-or-are-they-myth.

——. "Dogs Growl Honestly and Women Understand Better Than

Men." *Animal Emotions* (blog). *Psychology Today*, May 17, 2017. https://www.psychologytoday.com/us/blog/animal-emotions/201705 /dogs-growl-honestly-and-women-understand-better-men.

———. "Dogs Know When They've Been Dissed, and Don't Like It a Bit." *Animal Emotions* (blog). *Psychology Today*, July 23, 2014. https://www .psychologytoday.com/blog/animal-emotions/201407/dogs-know -when-theyve-been-dissed-and-dont-it-bit.

———. "Dogs Line Up with the Earth's Magnetic Field to Poop and Pee." *Animal Emotions* (blog). *Psychology Today*, January 2, 2014. https://www.psychologytoday.com/blog/animal-emotions/201401 /dogs-line-the-earths-magnetic-field-poop-and-pee.

———. "Dog Smarts: If We Were Smarter, We'd Understand Them Better." *Animal Emotions* (blog). *Psychology Today*, January 11, 2017. https://www.psychologytoday.com/blog/animal-emotions/201701 /dog-smarts-if-we-were-smarter-wed-understand-them-better.

———. "Do Our Dogs Really Love Us More Than Our Cats Do?" *Animal Emotions* (blog). *Psychology Today*, February 3, 2016. https://www .psychologytoday.com/blog/animal-emotions/201602/do-our-dogs -really-love-us-more-our-cats-do.

———. *The Emotional Lives of Animals*. Novato, CA: New World Library, 2007.

———. "'Gosh, My Dog Is Just Like Me': Shared Neuroticism." *Animal Emotions* (blog). *Psychology Today*, February 11, 2017. https://www .psychologytoday.com/blog/animal-emotions/201702/gosh-my-dog -is-just-me-shared-neuroticism.

———. "Hidden Tales of Yellow Snow: What a Dog's Nose Knows — Making Sense of Scents." *Animal Emotions* (blog). *Psychology Today*, June 29, 2009. https://www.psychologytoday.com/blog/animal -emotions/200906/hidden-tales-yellow-snow-what-dogs-nose -knows-making-sense-scents.

———. "A Hierarchy of Dog Needs: Abraham Maslow Meets the Mutts." *Animal Emotions* (blog). *Psychology Today*, May 31, 2017. https://www .psychologytoday.com/blog/animal-emotions/201705/hierarchy-dog -needs-abraham-maslow-meets-the-mutts.

———. "Hugging a Dog Is Just Fine When Done with Great Care."

Animal Emotions (blog). *Psychology Today*, April 28, 2016. https://
www.psychologytoday.com/blog/animal-emotions/201604/hugging
-dog-is-just-fine-when-done-great-care.

———. "iSpeakDog: A Website Devoted to Becoming Dog Literate." *Animal Emotions* (blog). *Psychology Today*, March 27, 2017. https://www
.psychologytoday.com/blog/animal-emotions/201703/ispeakdog
-website-devoted-becoming-dog-literate. An interview with Tracy
Krulik, founder of iSpeakDog.

———. *Minding Animals: Awareness, Emotions, and Heart.* New York:
Oxford University Press, 2002.

———. "Older Dogs: Giving Elder Canines Lots of Love and Good
Lives." *Animal Emotions* (blog). *Psychology Today*, December 1, 2016.
https://www.psychologytoday.com/blog/animal-emotions/201612
/older-dogs-giving-elder-canines-lots-love-and-good-lives.

———. "Perils of Pooping: Why Animals Don't Need Toilet Paper." *Animal Emotions* (blog). *Psychology Today*, January 14, 2014. https://www
.psychologytoday.com/blog/animal-emotions/201401/perils-pooping
-why-animals-dont-need-toilet-paper.

———. "Play Signals as Punctuation: The Structure of Social Play in
Canids." *Behaviour* 132 (1995): 419–29. http://cogprints.org/158/1
/199709003.html.

———. *Rewilding Our Hearts: Building Pathways of Compassion and
Coexistence.* Novato, CA: New World Library, 2014.

———. "Scent-Marking by Free Ranging Domestic Dogs: Olfactory and
Visual Components." *Biology of Behavior* 4 (1979): 123–39.

———, ed. *The Smile of a Dolphin: Remarkable Accounts of Animal Emotions.* Washington, DC: Discovery Books, 2000.

———. "Social Communication in Canids: Evidence for the Evolution
of a Stereotyped Mammalian Display." *Science* 197 (1977): 1097–99.
http://animalstudiesrepository.org/cgi/viewcontent.cgi?article
=1038&context=acwp_ena.

———. "Some Dogs Prefer Praise and a Belly Rub over Treats." *Animal
Emotions* (blog). *Psychology Today*, August 22, 2016. https://www
.psychologytoday.com/blog/animal-emotions/201608/some-dogs
-prefer-praise-and-belly-rub-over-treats.

———. "Training Dogs: Food Is Fine and Your Dog Will Still Love You." *Animal Emotions* (blog). *Psychology Today*, December 31, 2016. https://www.psychologytoday.com/blog/animal-emotions/201612 /training-dogs-food-is-fine-and-your-dog-will-still-love-you.

———. "Valuing Dogs More Than War Victims: Bridging the Empathy Gap." *Animal Emotions* (blog). *Psychology Today*, August 21, 2016. https://www.psychologytoday.com/blog/animal-emotions/201608 /valuing-dogs-more-war-victims-bridging-the-empathy-gap.

———. "We Don't Know If Dogs Feel Guilt, So Stop Saying They Don't." *Animal Emotions* (blog). *Psychology Today*, May 22, 2016. https:// www.psychologytoday.com/us/blog/animal-emotions/201605 /we-dont-know-if-dogs-feel-guilt-so-stop-saying-they-dont.

———. "What's Happening When Dogs Play Tug-of-War?: Dog Park Chatter." *Animal Emotions* (blog). *Psychology Today*, May 6, 2016. https://www.psychologytoday.com/us/blog/animal-emotions/201605 /whats-happening-when-dogs-play-tug-war-dog-park-chatter.

———. "Why Dogs Belong Off-Leash: It's Win-Win for All." *Animal Emotions* (blog). *Psychology Today*, May 25, 2016. https://www .psychologytoday.com/us/blog/animal-emotions/201605/why-dogs -belong-leash-its-win-win-all.

———. *Why Dogs Hump and Bees Get Depressed: The Fascinating Science of Animal Intelligence, Emotions, Friendship, and Conservation.* Novato, CA: New World Library, 2014.

———. "Why People Buy Dogs Who They Know Will Suffer and Die Young." *Animal Emotions* (blog). *Psychology Today*, February 25, 2017. https://www.psychologytoday.com/us/blog/animal-emotions/201702 /why-people-buy-dogs-who-they-know-will-suffer-and-die-young.

Bekoff, Marc, and Carron Meaney. "Interactions among Dogs, People, and the Environment in Boulder, Colorado: A Case Study." *Anthrozoös* 10 (1997): 23–31. http://www.aldog.org/wp-content/uploads/2011/04 /bekoff-meaney-1997-dogs.pdf.

Bekoff, Marc, and Jessica Pierce. *The Animals' Agenda: Freedom, Compassion, and Coexistence in the Human Age.* Boston: Beacon Press, 2017.

———. *Wild Justice: The Moral Lives of Animals.* Chicago: University of Chicago Press, 2009.

Ben-Aderet, Tobey, Mario Gallego-Abenza, David Reby, and Nicolas
    Mathevon. "Dog-Directed Speech: Why Do We Use It and Do Dogs
    Pay Attention to It?" *Proceedings of the Royal Society B* 284 (Jan-
    uary 11, 2017). http://rspb.royalsocietypublishing.org/content
    /284/1846/20162429.
Berns, Gregory. *How Dogs Love Us: A Neuroscientist and His Adopted Dog
    Decode the Canine Brain*. Boston: New Harvest, 2013.
———. *What It's Like to Be a Dog*. New York: Basic Books, 2017.
Berns, Gregory, Andrew Brooks, and Mark Spivak. "Scent of the Familiar:
    An fMRI Study of Canine Brain Responses to Familiar and Unfamil-
    iar Human and Dog Odors." *Behavioural Processes* 110 (2015): 37–46.
    http://www.sciencedirect.com/science/article/pii/s0376635714000473.
Bonanni, Roberto, Simona Cafazzo, Arianna Abis, Emanuela Barillari,
    Paola Valsecchi, and Eugenia Natoli. "Age-Graded Dominance
    Hierarchies and Social Tolerance in Packs of Free-Ranging Dogs."
    Behavioral Ecology (2017): 1004–20. https://academic.oup.com
    /beheco/article/28/4/1004/3743771.
Bonanni, Roberto, Eugenia Natoli, Simona Cafazzo, and Paola Valsecchi.
    "Free-Ranging Dogs Assess the Quantity of Opponents in Intergroup
    Conflicts." *Animal Cognition* 14 (2011): 103–15. http://link.springer
    .com/article/10.1007/s10071-010-0348-3.
Bonanni, Roberto, Paola Valsecchi, and Eugenia Natoli. "Pattern of
    Individual Participation and Cheating in Conflicts between Groups of
    Free-Ranging Dogs." *Animal Behaviour* 79 (2010): 957–68. http://www
    .sciencedirect.com/science/article/pii/s0003347210000382.
Bradshaw, John. *Dog Sense: How the New Science of Dog Behavior Can
    Make You a Better Friend to Your Pet*. New York: Basic Books, 2014.
Bradshaw, John, and Nicola Rooney. "Dog Social Behavior and Com-
    munication." In *The Domestic Dog: Its Evolution, Behavior and
    Interactions with People*, edited by James Serpell, 133–59. New York:
    Cambridge University Press, 2017.
Brandow, Michael. *A Matter of Breeding: A Biting History of Pedigree Dogs
    and How the Quest for Status Has Harmed Man's Best Friend*. Boston:
    Beacon Press, 2015.
Briggs, Helen. "Cats May Be as Intelligent as Dogs, Say Scientists." *BBC*

News, January 25, 2017. https://www.bbc.com/news/science-environment
-38665057.

Brophey, Kim. *Meet Your Dog*. San Francisco: Chronicle Books, 2018.

Brulliard, Karin. "In a First, Alaska Divorce Courts Will Now Treat Pets
More Like Children." *Animalia* (blog). *Washington Post*, January 24,
2017. https://www.washingtonpost.com/news/animalia/wp/2017
/01/24/in-a-first-alaska-divorce-courts-will-now-treat-pets-more
-like-children/?utm_term=.1ab12e0738a1.

Burghardt, Gordon. *The Genesis of Animal Play: Testing the Limits*.
Cambridge, MA: Bradford Books, 2005.

Byosiere, Sarah-Elizabeth, Julia Espinosa, and Barbara Smuts. "Investigating the Function of Play Bows in Adult Pet Dogs (*Canis lupus
familiaris*)." *Behavioural Processes* 125 (2016): 106–13. https://www
.researchgate.net/publication/295898387_investigating_the_function
_of_play_bows_in_adult_pet_dogs_canis_lupus_familiaris.

Cafazzo, Simona, Eugenia Natoli, and Paola Valsecchi. "Scent-Marking
Behaviour in a Pack of Free-Ranging Domestic Dogs." *Ethology* 118
(2012): 955–66. https://onlinelibrary.wiley.com/doi/abs/10.1111/j.1439
-0310.2012.02088.x.

Carlos, Naia. "Even Dogs Have Gotten into the Plastic Surgery Craze with
Botox, Nose Jobs, and More." *Nature World News*, March 22, 2017.
http://www.natureworldnews.com/articles/36610/20170322/even
-dogs-gotten-plastic-surgery-craze-botox-nose-jobs-more.htm.

———. "True Best Friends: Dogs, Humans Mirror Each Other's Personality." *Nature World News*, February 10, 2017. https://www.natureworld
news.com/articles/35563/20170210/true-best-friends-dogs-humans
-mirror-each-others-personality.htm.

Case, Linda. *Dog Smart*. Mahomet, IL: AutumnGold Publishing, 2018.

Cavalier, Darlene, and Eric Kennedy. *The Rightful Place of Science: Citizen
Science*. Tempe, AZ: Consortium for Science, Policy & Outcomes,
2016.

Chan, Melissa. "The Mysterious History behind Humanity's Love of
Dogs." *Time*, August 25, 2016. http://time.com/4459684/national
-dog-day-history-domestic-dogs-wolves.

Cherney, Elyssa. "Orange-Osceola State Attorney Creates Animal Cruelty

Unit." *Orlando Sentinel*, July 29, 2016. http://www.orlandosentinel
.com/news/os-state-attorney-specialty-unit-20160729-story.html.

"Clever Dog Steals Treats from Kitchen Counter." YouTube video, 1:52.
Posted by "Poke My Heart." June 14, 2012. https://www.youtube.com
/watch?v=xybbymuyfwq.

Cook, Gareth. "Inside the Dog Mind." *Mind* (blog). *Scientific American*,
May 1, 2013. http://www.scientificamerican.com/article/inside-the
-dog-mind.

Cook, Peter, Ashley Prichard, Mark Spivak, and Gregory S. Berns. "Awake
Canine fMRI Predicts Dogs' Preference for Praise versus Food."
Social Cognitive and Affective Neuroscience 11, no. 12 (2016): 1853–62.
https://doi.org/10.1093/scan/nsw102.

Coren, Stanley. "Are There Behavior Changes When Dogs Are Spayed or
Neutered?" *Canine Corner* (blog). *Psychology Today*, February 22,
2017. https://www.psychologytoday.com/blog/canine-corner/201702
/are-there-behavior-changes-when-dogs-are-spayed-or-neutered.

———. "A Designer Dog-Maker Regrets His Creation." *Canine Corner*
(blog). *Psychology Today*, April 1, 2014. https://www.psychologytoday
.com/blog/canine-corner/201404/designer-dog-maker-regrets-his
-creation.

———. "Do Dogs Have a Sense of Humor?" *Canine Corner* (blog). *Psychology Today*, December 17, 2015. https://www.psychologytoday.com
/blog/canine-corner/201512/do-dogs-have-sense-humor.

———. *How Dogs Think: What the World Looks Like to Them and Why
They Act the Way They Do*. New York: Atria Books, 2005.

———. "Long Tails Versus Short Tails and Canine Communication." *Canine Corner* (blog). *Psychology Today*, February 1, 2012. https://www
.psychologytoday.com/blog/canine-corner/201202/long-tails-versus
-short-tails-and-canine-communication.

———. "Understanding the Nature of Dog Intelligence." *Canine Corner*
(blog). *Psychology Today*, February 16, 2016. https://www.psychology
today.com/blog/canine-corner/201602/understanding-the-nature
-dog-intelligence.

———. "What Are Dogs Trying to Say When They Bark?" *Canine Corner*
(blog). *Psychology Today*, March 15, 2011. https://www.psychology

today.com/blog/canine-corner/201103/what-are-dogs-trying-say
-when-they-bark.

———. "What a Wagging Dog Tail Really Means: New Scientific
Data." *Canine Corner* (blog). *Psychology Today*, December 5, 2011.
https://www.psychologytoday.com/blog/canine-corner/201112/what
-wagging-dog-tail-really-means-new-scientific-data.

———. *The Wisdom of Dogs*. N.p.: Blue Terrier Press, 2014.

Dahl, Melissa. "What Does a Dog See in a Mirror?" *Science of Us* (blog).
New York, May 23, 2016. http://nymag.com/scienceofus/2016/05
/what-does-your-dog-see-when-he-looks-in-the-mirror.html.

Davis, Nicola. "Puppies' Response to Speech Could Shed Light on
Baby-Talk, Suggests Study." *Guardian*, January 10, 2017. https://www
.theguardian.com/science/2017/jan/11/puppies-response-to-speech
-could-shed-light-on-baby-talk-suggests-study.

Derr, Mark. *Dog's Best Friend: Annals of the Dog-Human Relationship*.
Chicago: University of Chicago Press, 2004.

———. *How the Dog Became the Dog: From Wolves to Our Best Friends*.
New York: Overlook Press, 2011.

———. "What Do Those Barks Mean? To Dogs, It's All Just Talk." *New
York Times*, April 24, 2001. http://www.nytimes.com/2001/04/24
/science/what-do-those-barks-mean-to-dogs-it-s-all-just-talk.html.

Dodman, Nicholas. *Pets on the Couch: Neurotic Dogs, Compulsive Cats,
Anxious Birds, and the New Science of Animal Psychiatry*. New York:
Atria Books, 2016.

"Dogs Share Food with Other Dogs Even in Complex Situations." *Science-
Daily*, January 27, 2017. https://www.sciencedaily.com/releases/2017
/01/170127112954.htm.

Donaldson, Jean. *Fight!: A Practical Guide to the Treatment of Dog-Dog
Aggression*. N.p.: Direct Book Service, 2002.

———. *Train Your Dog Like a Pro*. New York: Howell Book House, 2010.

Dunbar, Ian. *Before and After Getting Your Puppy*. Novato, CA: New World
Library, 2004.

El Nasser, Haya. "Fastest-Growing Urban Parks Are for the Dogs." *USA
Today*, December 8, 2011. http://usatoday30.usatoday.com/news
/nation/story/2011-12-07/dog-parks/51715340/1.

Fagen, Robert. *Animal Play Behavior*. New York: Oxford University Press, 1981.

Fallon, Melissa, and Vickie Davenport. *Babies, Kids and Dogs*. United Kingdom: Veloce Publishing, 2016.

Farricelli, Adrienne. "Does Human Perfume Affect Dogs?" Cuteness. https://www.cuteness.com/blog/content/does-human-perfume -affect-dogs.

Feddersen-Petersen, and Dorit Urd. "Vocalization of European Wolves (*Canis lupus lupus L.*) and Various Dog Breeds (*Canis lupus f. fam.*)." *Archiv für Tierzucht* 43 (2000): 387–97. https://www.arch-anim-breed .net/43/387/2000/aab-43-387-2000.pdf.

Feuerbacher, E.N., and C.D. Wynne. "Most Domestic Dogs (*Canis lupus familiaris*) Prefer Food to Petting: Population, Context, and Schedule Effects in Concurrent Choice." *Journal of the Experimental Analysis of Behavior* 101 (2014): 385–405. https://www.ncbi.nlm.nih.gov/pubmed /24643871.

Fox, Michael W. *Behaviour of Wolves, Dogs, and Related Canids*. New York: Harper & Row, 1972.

———. *Integrative Development of Brain and Behavior in the Dog*. Chicago: University of Chicago Press, 1971.

Fugazza, Claudia, Ákos Pogány, and Ádám Miklósi. "Recall of Others' Actions after Incidental Encoding Reveals Episodic-like Memory in Dogs." *Current Biology* 26 (2016): 3209–13. http://dx.doi.org/10.1016 /j.cub.2016.09.057.

Fukuzawa, Megumi, and Ayano Hashi. "Can We Estimate Dogs' Recognition of Objects in Mirrors from Their Behavior and Response Time?" *Journal of Veterinary Behavior* 17 (2017): 1–5. http://dx.doi.org/10.1016 /j.jveb.2016.10.008.

Gatti, Roberto Cazzolla. "Self-Consciousness: Beyond the Looking-Glass and What Dogs Found There." *Ethology Ecology and Evolution* 28 (2016): 232–40. https://www.tandfonline.com/doi/full/10.1080/039493 70.2015.1102777.

Gaunet, F., E. Pari-Perrin, and G. Bernardin. "Description of Dogs and Owners in Outdoor Built-Up Areas and Their More-Than-Human

Issues." *Environmental Management* 54, no. 3 (2014): 383–401. doi: 10.1007/s00267-014-0297-8.

Gayomali, Chris. "Dogs Might Poop in Line with the Earth's Magnetic Field." The Week, January 2, 2014. http://theweek.com/articles /453642/dogs-might-poop-line-earths-magnetic-field.

Geggel, Laura. "Anxiety May Give Dogs Gray Hair." *Live Science*, December 19, 2016. http://www.livescience.com/57254-anxiety-may-give -dogs-gray-hair.html.

Gill, Victoria, and Jonathan Webb. "Dogs 'Can Tell Difference between Happy and Angry Faces.'" *BBC News*, February 12, 2015. http://www .bbc.com/news/science-environment-31384525.

Gough, William, and Betty McGuire. "Urinary Posture and Motor Laterality in Dogs (*Canis lupus familiaris*) at Two Shelters." *Applied Animal Behaviour Science* 168 (2015): 61–70. http://www.appliedanimal behaviour.com/article/s0168-1591(15)00120-3/abstract?cc=y=.

Griffin, Donald. *The Question of Animal Awareness*. 1976. Reprint, New York: Rockefeller University Press, 1981.

Griffiths, Sarah. "Dogs Snub People Who Are Mean to Their Owners — and Even Reject Their Treats." *Daily Mail*, June 13, 2015. http://www .dailymail.co.uk/sciencetech/article-3121280/dogs-snub-people -mean-owners-reject-treats.html.

Grimm, David. *Citizen Canine: Our Evolving Relationship with Cats and Dogs*. New York: PublicAffairs, 2014.

Grossman, Anna Jane. "All Dog, No Bark: The Pitfalls of Devocalization Surgery." *The Blog* (blog). *HuffPost*, November 20, 2012. http://www .huffingtonpost.com/anna-jane-grossman/debarking_b_2160971 .html.

Gruen, Lori, ed. *The Ethics of Captivity*. New York: Oxford University Press, 2014.

Hallgren, Anders. *Ethics and Ethology for a Happy Dog*. Richmond, UK: Cadmos Publishing Limited, 2015.

Handelman, Barbara. *Canine Behavior: A Photo Illustrated Handbook*. Wenatchee, WA: Dogwise Publishing, 2008.

Hare, Brian, and Vanessa Woods. *The Genius of Dogs: How Dogs Are Smarter Than You Think*. New York: Plume, 2013.

Harris, Christine, and Caroline Prouvost. "Jealousy in Dogs." *PLOS One* 9, no. 7 (2014). http://journals.plos.org/plosone/article?id=10.1371/journal.pone.0094597.

Hathaway, Bill. "Dogs Ignore Bad Advice That Humans Follow." *YaleNews*, September 26, 2016. http://news.yale.edu/2016/09/26/dogs-ignore-bad-advice-humans-follow.

Hecht, Julie. "Dog Speak: The Sounds of Dogs." *The Bark* 73 (Spring 2013). http://thebark.com/content/dog-speak-sounds-dogs.

———. "Why Do Dogs Roll Over During Play?" *Dog Spies* (blog). *Scientific American*, January 9, 2015. http://blogs.scientificamerican.com/dog-spies/why-do-dogs-roll-over-during-play.

Hekman, Jessica. "Understanding Canine Social Hierarchies." *The Bark* 84 (Winter 2015). http://thebark.com/content/understanding-canine-social-hierarchies.

Hirskyj-Douglas, Ilyena. "Here's What Dogs See When They Watch Television." The Conversation, September 8, 2016. https://theconversation.com/heres-what-dogs-see-when-they-watch-television-65000.

Horowitz, Alexandra. "Attention to Attention in Domestic Dog (*Canis familiaris*) Dyadic Play." *Animal Cognition* 12, no. 1 (2009): 107–18.

———. *Being a Dog: Following the Dog into a World of Smell*. New York: Scribner, 2016.

———. "Disambiguating the 'Guilty Look': Salient Prompts to a Familiar Dog Behavior." *Behavioural Processes* 81, (2009): 447–52.

———, ed. *Domestic Dog Cognition and Behavior: The Scientific Study of Canis familiaris*. New York: Springer, 2014.

Horowitz, Alexandra, and Marc Bekoff. "Naturalizing Anthropomorphism: Behavioral Prompts to Our Humanizing of Animals." *Anthrozoös* 20 (2007): 23–35.

Horwitz, Debra F., J. Ciribassi, and Steve Dale, eds. *Decoding Your Dog: The Ultimate Experts Explain Common Dog Behaviors and Reveal How to Prevent or Change Unwanted Ones*. Boston: Houghton Mifflin Harcourt, 2014.

Howard, Jacqueline. "Here's More Proof That Dogs Can Totally Read Our Facial Expressions." *HuffPost*, February 13, 2015. http://www

.huffingtonpost.com/2015/02/13/dogs-read-faces-study-video_n
_6672422.html.

Hrala, Josh. "Your Dog Doesn't Trust You When You're Angry, Study
Finds." *Science Alert.* May 24, 2016. http://www.sciencealert.com
/your-dog-doesn-t-trust-you-when-you-re-angry-study-finds.

Huber, Ludwig. "How Dogs Perceive and Understand Us." *Current Directions in Psychological Science* 25, no. 5 (2016). http://journals.sagepub
.com/doi/abs/10.1177/0963721416656329.

Irvine, Leslie. *If You Tame Me: Understanding Our Connection with Animals.* Philadelphia: Temple University Press, 2004.

Johnson, Rebecca, Alan Beck, and Sandra McCune, eds. *The Health
Benefits of Dog Walking for People and Pets: Evidence and Case Studies.*
West Lafayette, IN: Purdue University Press, 2011.

Kaminski, Juliane, and Sarah Marshall-Pescini, eds. *The Social Dog:
Behavior and Cognition.* New York: Academic Press, 2014.

Kaminski, Juliane, and Marie Nitzschner. "Do Dogs Get the Point?: A
Review of Dog–Human Communication Ability." *Learning and Motivation* 44 (2013): 294–302. http://www.sciencedirect.com/science
/article/pii/s0023969013000325.

Käufer, Mechtild. *Canine Play Behavior: The Science of Dogs at Play.*
Wenatchee, WA: Dogwise Publishing, 2014.

King, Camille, Thomas J. Smith, Temple Grandin, and Peter Borchelt.
"Anxiety and Impulsivity: Factors Associated with Premature Gray-
ing in Young Dogs." *Applied Animal Behaviour Science* 185 (2016):
78–85. http://www.appliedanimalbehaviour.com/article/s0168-1591
(16)30277-5/abstract?cc=y=.

Klonsky, Jane Sobel. *Unconditional: Older Dogs, Deeper Love.* Washington,
DC: National Geographic, 2016.

Krulik, Tracy. "Dogs and Dominance: Let's Change the Conversation."
Dogz and Their Peoplez (blog), January 18, 2017. http://dogzandtheir
peoplez.com/2017/01/18/dogs-and-dominance-lets-change-the
-conversation.

———. "Dominance and Dogs: The Push-ups Challenge." *Dogz and Their
Peoplez* (blog), January 16, 2017. http://dogzandtheirpeoplez
.com/2017/01/16/dominance-and-dogs-the-push-ups-challenge.

————. "Are Dogs Really Eager to Please?" *The Bark* 88 (Winter 2016), 39–42, per thebark.com.

Kuroshima, Hika, Yukari Nabeoka, Yusuke Hori, Hitomi Chijiiwa, and Kazuo Fujita. "Experience Matters: Dogs (*Canis familiaris*) Infer Physical Properties of Objects from Movement Clues." *Behavioural Processes* 136 (2017): 54–58. http://www.sciencedirect.com/science /article/pii/s037663571630208x.

"Learning to Speak Dog Part 4: Reading a Dog's Body." *Tails from the Lab* (blog). August 29, 2012. http://www.tailsfromthelab.com/2012/08/29 /learning-to-speak-dog-part-4-reading-a-dogs-body.

Lewis, Susan. "The Meaning of Dog Barks." *NOVA*, October 28, 2010. http://www.pbs.org/wgbh/nova/nature/meaning-dog-barks.html.

London, Karen. "Should We Call These Canine Behaviors Calming Signals?" *The Bark*, June 2, 2017. http://thebark.com/content/should -we-call-these-canine-behaviors-calming-signals.

"A Man's Best Friend: Study Shows Dogs Can Recognize Human Emotions." *ScienceDaily*, January 12, 2016. https://www.sciencedaily.com /releases/2016/01/160112214507.htm.

Mariti, Chiara, et al. "Analysis of the Intraspecific Visual Communication in the Domestic Dog (*Canis familiaris*): A Pilot Study on the Case of Calming Signals." *Journal of Veterinary Behavior* 18 (2017): 49–55. http://www.journalvetbehavior.com/article/s1558-7878(16)30246-5 /abstract.

Martino, Marissa. *Human/Canine Behavior Connection: A Better Self through Dog Training*. Boulder, CO: CreateSpace Independent Publishing Platform, 2017.

McArthur, Jo-Anne. *Captive*. New York: Lantern Books, 2017.

McConnell, Patricia. *For the Love of a Dog: Understanding Emotion in You and Your Best Friend*. New York: Ballantine Books, 2009.

————. "A New Look at Play Bows." *The Other End of the Leash* (blog), March 28, 2016. http://www.patriciamcconnell.com/theotherendof theleash/a-new-look-at-play-bows.

Michaels, Linda. *Do No Harm: Dog Training and Behavior Manual*. 2017. https://gumroad.com/lindamichaels.

———. "Hierarchy of Dog Needs." Del Mar Dog Training. http://www
.dogpsychologistoncall.com/hierarchy-of-dog-needs-tm.

Miklósi, Ádám. *Dog Behaviour, Evolution, and Cognition*. New York: Oxford University Press, 2016.

Miller, Pat. "5 Steps to Deal with Dog Growling." *Whole Dog Journal*, October 2009. Updated March 13, 2018. http://www.whole-dog-journal
.com/issues/12_10/features/dealing-with-dog-growling_16163-1.html.

———. *Play with Your Dog*. Wenatchee, WA: Doggies Training Manual,
2008.

———. *The Power of Positive Dog Training*. Nashville, TN: Howell Book
House, 2008.

Morey, Darcy. *Dogs: Domestication and the Development of a Social Bond*.
New York: Cambridge University Press, 2010.

"Most Desirable Traits in Dogs for Potential Adopters." *ScienceDaily*,
November 3, 2016. https://www.sciencedaily.com/releases/2016/11
/161103151956.htm.

Müller, Corsin A., Kira Schmitt, Anjuli L. A. Barber, and Ludwig Huber.
"Dogs Can Discriminate Emotional Expressions of Human Faces."
Current Biology 25, no. 5 (March 2015): 601–5. http://www.cell.com
/current-biology/abstract/s0960-9822(14)01693-5.

Nagasawa, Miho, Emi Kawai, Kazutaka Mogi, and Takefumi Kikusui.
"Dogs Show Left Facial Lateralization upon Reunion with Their
Owners." *Behavioural Processes* 98 (2013): 112–16. http://www.science
direct.com/science/article/pii/s0376635713001101.

Olson, Marie-Louise. "Dogs Have Feelings Too!: Neuroscientist Reveals
Research That Our Canine Friends Have Emotions Just Like Us."
Daily Mail, October 6, 2013. http://www.dailymail.co.uk/news/article
-2447991/dogs-feelings-neuroscientist-reveals-research-canine
-friends-emotions-just-like-us.html#ixzz4ghizfcad.

Overall, Christine, ed. *Pets and People: The Ethics of Our Relationships with
Companion Animals*. New York: Oxford University Press, 2017.

Overall, Karen. *Manual of Clinical Behavioral Medicine for Dogs and Cats*.
St. Louis: Elsevier Mosby, 2013.

Pachniewska, Amanda. "List of Animals That Have Passed the Mirror

Test." *Animal Cognition*, April 15, 2015. http://www.animalcognition
.org/2015/04/15/list-of-animals-that-have-passed-the-mirror-test.

Palagi, Elisabetta, Velia Nicotra, and Giada Cordoni. "Rapid Mimicry and
Emotional Contagion in Domestic Dogs." *Royal Society Open Science*,
December 2015. http://rsos.royalsocietypublishing.org/content/2/12
/150505.

Pangal, Sindhoor. "Lives of Streeties: A Study on the Activity Budget of
Free-Ranging Dogs." *IAABC Journal*, Winter 2017. https://winter2017
.iaabcjournal.org/lives-of-streeties-a-study-on-the-activity-budget
-of-free-ranging-dogs.

Paxton, David. *Why It's OK to Talk to Your Dog: Co-Evolution of People and
Dogs*. N.p.: printed by author, 2011.

Payne, Elyssa M., Pauleen C. Bennett, and Paul D. McGreevy. "DogTube:
An Examination of Dogmanship Online." *Journal of Veterinary Behavior* 17 (2017): 50–61. http://www.journalvetbehavior.com/article
/s1558-7878(16)30167-8/abstract.

Pellis, Sergio, and Vivien Pellis. *The Playful Brain: Venturing to the Limits
of Neuroscience*. London: Oneworld Publications, 2010.

Penkowa, Milena. *Dogs and Human Health: The New Science of Dog Therapy and Therapy Dogs*. Bloomington, IN: Balboa Press, 2015.

Petty, Michael. *Dr. Petty's Pain Relief for Dogs: The Complete Medical and
Integrative Guide to Treating Pain*. Woodstock, VT: Countryman
Press, 2016.

Pierce, Jessica. "Deciding When a Pet Has Suffered Enough." *Sunday Review* (opinion). *New York Times*, September 22, 2012. http://www
.nytimes.com/2012/09/23/opinion/sunday/deciding-when-a-pet
-has-suffered-enough.html.

———. "Is Your Dog in Pain?" *All Dogs Go to Heaven* (blog). *Psychology
Today*, February 3, 2016. https://www.psychologytoday.com/blog
/all-dogs-go-heaven/201602/is-your-dog-in-pain.

———. "Is Your Pet Lonely and Bored?" *New York Times*, May 7, 2016.

———. *The Last Walk: Reflections on Our Pets at the End of Their Lives*.
Chicago: University of Chicago Press, 2012.

———. "Not Just Walking the Dog: What a Dog Walk Can Tell Us about
Our Human-Animal Relationships." *All Dogs Go to Heaven* (blog).

Psychology Today, March 16, 2017. https://www.psychologytoday.com /blog/all-dogs-go-heaven/201703/not-just-walking-the-dog.

———. "Palliative Care for Pets." Seniors Resource Guide. November 2012. http://www.seniorsresourceguide.com/articles/art01240.html.

———. *Run, Spot, Run: The Ethics of Keeping Pets*. Chicago: University of Chicago Press, 2016.

Pierotti, Ray, and Brandy Fogg. *The First Domestication: How Wolves and Humans Coevolved*. New Haven: Yale University Press, 2017.

Pongrácz, P., C. Molnár, A. Miklósi, and V. Csányi. "Human Listeners Are Able to Classify Dog (*Canis familiaris*) Barks Recorded in Different Situations." *Journal of Comparative Psychology* 119, no. 2 (2005): 136–44. doi: 10.1037/0735-7036.119.2.136.

Quenqua, Douglas. "A Dog's Tail Wag Says a Lot, to Other Dogs." *New York Times*, October 31, 2013. http://www.nytimes.com/2013/11/05 /science/a-dogs-tail-wag-can-say-a-lot.html.

Ray, C. Claiborne. "How Does One Dog Recognize Another as a Dog?" *New York Times*, February 15, 2016. http://www.nytimes.com/2016 /02/16/science/how-does-one-dog-recognize-another-as-a-dog .html?_r=1.

Reid, Pamela. *Dog Insight*. Wenatchee, WA: Dogwise Publishing, 2011.

Reisner, Ilana. "The Learning Dog: A Discussion of Training Methods." In *The Domestic Dog: Its Evolution, Behavior and Interactions with People*, edited by James Serpell, 210–26. New York: Cambridge University Press, 2017.

Rian, Sian, and Helen Zuich. *No Walks? No Worries: Maintaining Wellbeing in Dogs on Restricted Exercise*. United Kingdom: Veloce Publishing, 2014.

Riley, Katherine. "Puppy Love: The Coddling of the American Pet." *The Atlantic*, May 2017. https://www.theatlantic.com/magazine/archive /2017/05/puppy-love/521442.

Rosell, Frank Narve. *Secrets of the Snout: The Dog's Incredible Nose*. Chicago: University of Chicago Press, 2018.

Rose-Solomon, Diane. *What to Expect When Adopting a Dog: A Guide to Successful Dog Adoption for Every Family*. N.p.: SP03 Publishing, 2016.

Rugaas, Turid. *On Talking Terms with Dogs: Calming Signals*. Wenatchee, WA: Dogwise Publishing, 2006.

Sanders, Clinton. *Understanding Dogs: Living and Working with Canine Companions*. Philadelphia: Temple University Press, 1998.

Scott, John Paul, and John Fuller. *Genetics and the Social Behavior of the Dog*. 1965. Reprint, Chicago: University of Chicago Press, 1998.

Scully, Marisa. "The Westminster Dog Show Fails the Animals It Profits From: Here's Why." *Guardian*, February 16, 2017. https://www.theguardian.com/sport/2017/feb/16/the-westminster-dog-show-fails-the-animals-it-profits-from-heres-why.

Serpell, James. "Creatures of the Unconscious: Companion Animals as Mediators." In *Companion Animals and Us: Exploring the Relationships between People and Pets*, edited by Anthony Podberscek, Elizabeth Paul, and James Serpell, 108–21. New York: Cambridge University Press, 2005.

———, ed. *The Domestic Dog: Its Evolution, Behavior and Interactions with People*. New York: Cambridge University Press, 2017.

Shyan, Melissa R., Kristina A. Fortune, and Christine King. "'Bark Parks': A Study on Interdog Aggression in a Limited-Control Environment." *Journal of Applied Animal Welfare Science* 6, no. 1 (2003): 25–32. http://freshairtraining.com/pdfs/barkparks.pdf.

Siler, Wes. "Why Dogs Belong Off-Leash in the Outdoors." *Outside*, May 24, 2016. http://www.outsideonline.com/2082546/why-dogs-belong-leash-outdoors.

Smuts, Barbara, Erika Bauer, and Camille Ward. "Rollovers during Play: Complementary Perspectives." *Behavioural Processes* 116 (2015): 50–52. http://www.sciencedirect.com/science/article/pii/s0376635715001047.

Špinka, Marek, Ruth Newberry, and Marc Bekoff. "Mammalian Play: Training for the Unexpected." *Quarterly Review of Biology* 76 (2001): 141–68. https://www.ncbi.nlm.nih.gov/pubmed/11409050.

Stewart, Laughlin, et al. "Citizen Science as a New Tool in Dog Cognition Research." *PLOS One* 10, no. 9 (2015). http://journals.plos.org/plosone/article?id=10.1371/journal.pone.0135176.

Stilwell, Victoria. *The Secret Language of Dogs*. Berkeley, CA: Ten Speed Press, 2016.

Sweet, Laurel J. "Teen Files Bill to Make Vocal Surgery Illegal." *Boston Herald*, February 2, 2009. http://www.bostonherald.com/news _opinion/local_coverage/2009/02/teen_files_bill_make_vocal_surgery _illegal.

Tenzin-Dolma, Lisa. *Dog Training: The Essential Guide*. Peterborough, UK: Need2Know, 2012.

Todd, Zazie. "'Dominance' Training Deprives Dogs of Positive Experiences." *Companion Animal Psychology* (blog). February 15, 2017. http://www.companionanimalpsychology.com/2017/02/dominance -training-deprives-dogs-of.html.

———. "New Literature Review Recommends Reward-Based Training." *Companion Animal Psychology* (blog). April 5, 2017. https://www .companionanimalpsychology.com/2017/04/new-literature-review -recommends-reward.html.

———. "What Is Positive Punishment in Dog Training?" *Companion Animal Psychology* (blog), October 25, 2017. https://www.companion-animal psychology.com/2017/10/what-is-positive-punishment-in-dog.html.

Vaira, Angelo, and Valeria Raimondi. *Un cuore felice: L'arte di giocare con il tuo cane [A Happy Heart: The Art of Playing with a Dog]*. Milan: Sperling & Kupfer, 2016.

Valeri, Robin Maria. "Tails of Laughter: A Pilot Study Examining the Relationship between Companion Animal Guardianship (Pet Ownership) and Laughter." *Society and Animals* 14, no. 3 (2006): 275–93. http://www.animalsandsociety.org/wp-content/uploads/2016/04 /valeri.pdf.

Vollmer, Peter. "Do Mischievous Dogs Reveal Their 'Guilt'?" *Veterinary Medicine / Small Animal Clinician* (June 1977): 1002–5.

Ward, Camille, Rebecca Trisko, and Barbara Smuts. "Third-Party Interventions in Dyadic Play between Littermates of Domestic Dogs, *Canis lupus familiaris*." *Animal Behaviour* 78 (2009): 1153–60. http://pawsoflife-org.k9handleracademy.com/library/behavior/ward _2009.pdf.

Warden, C. J., and L. H. Warner. "The Sensory Capacities and Intelligence of Dogs, with a Report on the Ability of the Noted Dog 'Fellow' to

Respond to Verbal Stimuli." *Quarterly Review of Biology* 3 (1928): 1–28. http://www.journals.uchicago.edu/doi/abs/10.1086/394292.

Wild, Karen. *Being a Dog.* Buffalo, NY: Firefly Books, 2016.

Wogan, Lisa. *Dog Park Wisdom: Real-World Advice on Choosing, Caring For, and Understanding Your Canine Companion.* Seattle: Skipstone Press, 2008.

Yin, Sophia. *How to Behave so Your Dog Behaves.* Neptune, NJ: THF Publications, 2010.

York, Tripp. *The End of Captivity? A Primate's Reflections on Zoos, Conservation, and Christian Ethics.* Eugene, OR: Cascade Books, 2015.

Ziv, Gal. "The Effects of Using Aversive Training Methods in Dogs: A Review." *Journal of Veterinary Behavior* 19 (2017): 50–60. http://www.journalvetbehavior.com/article/s1558-7878(17)30035-7/abstract.

Zulch, Helen, and Daniel Mills. *Life Skills for Puppies.* United Kingdom: Veloce Publishing, 2012.

Index

salivation and, 161–62n9; self-
recognition through, 25, 159n9;
taste sense as assistor of, 59–60;
visual acuity and, 111; of water, 64.
See also sniffing
smells (odors): aversive stimuli,
34; as composite signal, 116;
dog breath, 53; in dog-human
communication, 121; familiar, and
new environments, 49; in human
communication, 120–21; stink,
rolling in, 47–48
"smiling," 146
Snellen fraction, 109
sniffing: allowing, 44–45; dog-dog interaction and, 94, 96; information
collected from, 42; of pee spots,
45–47; touch sense and, 79
snuggling, 101
socialization: dog-dog interaction
and, 92–93; need for, 12; play and,
142, 143; of puppies, 137; to scary
noises, 137; touch aversions and,
79–80; vision loss and, 111
Society for the Prevention of Cruelty
to Animals (SPCA), 81
sounds: during alone times, 138; aversive stimuli, 34, 127–28, 134–36;
phobias involving, 134–37
sour (taste), 63
space, personal, 99–100
Špinka, Marek, 143–44
splitters, 21–22
standing over, 21
starches, digesting of, 57
St. Bernards, 67
strangers, 98, 99
stress, 34, 70–71, 98, 104, 129–30,
136–37
Sweden, 82
sweet (taste), 63
Switzerland, 82
sympathetic nervous system, 112

table scraps, 75
tag silencers, 136
tail position, 21, 112
tails, 114–16
taste: chewing behaviors and, 76–78;
composite signals and, 35; drooling and, 66–68, 161–62n9; gross
stuff and, 60–63; human vs. canine experiences of, 55–56, 63–64;
play and, 139; smell sense assisted
by, 59–60; of water, 64–65. *See also*
eating behaviors; food
taste buds, 55
taste receptors, 63–64
teeth, baring of, 130–31
television, as dog entertainment, 138
Ten Freedoms, 11
Ten Ways to Make Your Dog Happier
and More Content, 150
terEllen, Marije, 52
terriers, Boston, 117
theory of mind, 121
thirst, freedom from, 11
thunder, 136, 137
time, canine sense of, 43, 95, 104–5
Todd, Zazie, 81–82
"together time," 103–7, 138, 150
toilet, drinking from, 65
Tommy (dog), 64
tongue, 59, 60
tonguing, 60
tooth brushing, 53
tooth damage, 63
tooth decay, 53
touch: affection displays, 100–101;
aversion to, 79–80, 98–99; composite signals and, 35; consent involved in, 80; dog-dog interaction
and, 94; drooling and, 67; human
vs. canine experiences of, 79–80;
petting, 97–99; play and, 79, 139.
See also walks
Townsend, Susan, 4

About the Authors

Marc Bekoff is professor emeritus of ecology and evolutionary biology at the University of Colorado, Boulder. A fellow of the Animal Behavior Society, a recipient of their Exemplar Award for long-term significant contributions to the field of animal behavior, and a former Guggenheim Fellow, he has written and edited more than thirty books, the latest being *The Animals' Agenda: Freedom, Compassion, and Coexistence in the Human Age* and *Canine Confidential: Why Dogs Do What They Do*. Marc was presented with the Bank One Faculty Community Service Award in 2005 for the work he has done with children, senior citizens, and inmates, much of which continues today. In 2009 he was granted the St. Francis of Assisi Award by the New Zealand SPCA, and in 1986 Marc became the first American to win his age-class at the Tour du Haut Var bicycle race (also called the Master's/age-graded Tour de France). His homepage is marcbekoff.com.

Jessica Pierce is an affiliate faculty at the Center for Bioethics and Humanities, University of Colorado Anschutz Medical School. She is the author of nine books, including

The Last Walk: Reflections on Our Pets at the End of Their Lives and *Run, Spot, Run: The Ethics of Keeping Pets*, and she has published essays in the *New York Times*, the *Wall Street Journal*, and the *Guardian* and is a regular contributor to *Psychology Today*. Her homepage is jessicapierce.net.